# The Spokesman
## European Nuclear Disarmament
### Edited by Tony Simpson

Published by Spokesman for the
Bertrand Russell Peace Foundation
Ken Coates: Editor 1970 to 2010

**Spokesman 142**                    **2019**

## CONTENTS

Cover: European Nuclear Disarmament (1983), Peter Kennard

ISSN 1367 7748          ISBN 978 0 85124 8806

**Subscriptions**
Institutions £40.00 (ex UK)
£33.00 (UK)
Individuals £20.00 (UK)
£25.00 (ex UK)

A CIP catalogue record
for this book is available
from the British Library

**Published by**
The Bertrand Russell Peace
Foundation Ltd,
5 Churchill Park,
Nottingham, NG4 2HF
England
Tel. 0115 9708318
email:
editor@russfound.org
www.spokesmanbooks.com
www.russfound.org

**FSC**
**Mixed Sources**
Product group from well-managed
forests and other controlled sources

Cert no. SGS-COC-006541
www.fsc.org
© 1996 Forest Stewardship Council

**Editorial**

# European Nuclear Disarmament

For a decade from 1982, *The Spokesman* journal became *ENDpapers* and often chronicled the END Conventions that moved around Europe from Brussels to Berlin to Perugia to Amsterdam, Paris and onwards. The founding European Nuclear Disarmament Appeal had included a call for a representative conference of signatories to explore how to remove nuclear weapons from Europe. Eventually, Presidents Gorbachev and Reagan got the message and the Intermediate-range Nuclear Forces (INF) Treaty was signed in 1987, banning an entire class of nuclear weapons. Nevertheless, the United States continues to position nuclear bombs at airfields in Belgium, Germany, Italy, The Netherlands and Turkey, under auspices of its nuclear-armed NATO alliance.

Now, President Trump has announced that the United States is withdrawing from the INF Treaty, and President Putin quickly followed suit. **Katarzyna Kubiak,** in evidence to the UK Parliament, sets out why the Treaty matters, and what may be the consequences of its demise. For more than 30 years, the INF Treaty has been a pillar of nuclear security in Europe. Now it is being pulled down, without consultation of those countries most directly affected. In Romania, Russia's close neighbour on the Black Sea, the European Union's High Representative, Federica Mogherini, remarked that

> 'What we definitely do not want to see is our continent going back to being a battlefield or a place where other superpowers confront themselves. This belongs to a faraway history that both the INF Treaty and also the European Union as such have contributed to overcome once and for all.'

**Joseph Gerson** charts some of this 'faraway history', while Ambassador **Vladimir Chizhov** sketches Russia's current view of the wider international order. Commander **Robert Green** probes how the UK might constructively respond to the growing nuclear deterrence and disarmament crisis.

◄ European Nuclear Disarmament (1983), Peter Kennard

For its part, in a wide-ranging resolution 'on the future of the INF Treaty and the impact on the EU', the European Parliament

> 'Commends the entry into force of the UN Treaty on the Prohibition of Nuclear Weapons, the universalisation of the Non-Proliferation Treaty, and the establishment of further nuclear-free zones as positive steps … '

Europe's nuclear-weapons-free zone will surely stand high on the agenda of our renewed pursuit of European Nuclear Disarmament. We will make a start in Brussels in the autumn (see page 78).

\* \* \*

## Faraway History?

*Remarks by High Representative/Vice-President Federica Mogherini at the press conference following the informal meeting of the EU Defence Ministers in Bucharest on 31 January 2019*

**Q. Was the Intermediate-Range Nuclear Forces [INF] Treaty discussed this morning? We expect the United States to announce its withdrawal this afternoon. What does that mean for European security? In the discussion on China, was there any talk of how to persuade Beijing to participate in this kind of arms control?**

We did not discuss this at our meeting but obviously, as so many Foreign Ministers were gathered in the same room, this was an issue for discussion informally, bilaterally with some of them. As you might have heard, we discussed this with the Defence Ministers Wednesday night here in Bucharest, together also with the NATO Secretary-General Jens Stoltenberg, and I already had on Wednesday the opportunity of saying publicly what I would reiterate here: European countries and the European Union as such are not parties to the INF [Treaty] but Europe has been probably the one that has benefited the most from this Treaty that we have valued enormously, that we value enormously. Our wish and our call is for this Treaty to be preserved with full compliance by both parties and you know where the issue stands there. We are working on a common declaration at 28 [EU Member States] that might be released in the coming hours.

**Q. The United States' withdrawal from the INF Treaty was based on Russia's non-compliance with the agreement. What is the EU's official position on this fact?**

The European Union as the Union relies on the information that Member States share, including on this issue. As I had the opportunity of discussing many times, including during the NATO ministerial [meetings] and in the NATO headquarters in the last months, we have also had access to some of the information that NATO has shared with us. For the European Union – and then obviously Member States have direct sources of information and I am sure that especially those that are also NATO members or NATO allies might respond to this question also in their capacity as a NATO ally, which is true for the vast majority of the European Union Member States – what would be extremely important to see is full compliance with the INF Treaty and the preservation of the Treaty as a framework.

This is fully coherent not only with the security interests that Europe has. What we definitely do not want to see is our continent going back to being a battlefield or a place where other superpowers confront themselves. This belongs to a faraway history that both the INF Treaty and also the European Union as such have contributed to overcome once and for all. We definitely do not want to even consider the possibility of going backwards along this path, but this is also consistent with our overall approach that, we believe, is essential for the security of the world, and in particular an arms control architecture that is based on international treaties and multilateral treaties.

\* \* \*

'We are dangerously close to a world without arms control agreements, which would increase the risk of nuclear use'

*House of Lords Select Committee on International Relations, April 2019*

# The hour is getting late

*Joseph Gerson*

*Joseph Gerson of the American Friends Service Committee and the Campaign for Peace, Disarmament and Common Security addressed an international conference on 'Growing nuclear risks in a changing world' in New York in May 2019, which coincided with the ill-starred NPT Preparatory Committee.*

*So let us not talk falsely now*
*The hour is getting late*

Bob Dylan

The Intermediate-range Nuclear Forces Treaty came into force in 1987, bringing the Cold War to an end before the Berlin Wall was breached and the Soviet empire collapsed. The Treaty requires elimination and permanent renunciation of future deployment of all US and Russian nuclear and conventional ground-launched cruise and ballistic missiles with ranges of 300 to 3,500 miles. It greatly reduced (but did not eliminate) the danger of Europe becoming the initial theatre and victim of a US-Soviet apocalyptic nuclear war.

In October 2018, President Trump announced his plans to withdraw the United States from the Treaty, creating the political and strategic environment that is fuelling an unrestrained and extremely dangerous nuclear arms race. Trump is an inveterate liar. The *New York Times* reports that he just notched his 10,000 recorded lie since coming to office. But there are times when he should be taken at his word. He was not fooling when he boasted that 'we have more money than anyone else' and said 'let there be an arms race'. President Putin, in turn, threatened to match any new US missile deployments in Europe. And, with the New START (Strategic Arms Reduction) Treaty unlikely to be extended [beyond 2021], and given the disastrous record of US-Russian relations of the last decade, we are in the early stages of a US-Russian confrontation analogous to the Cold War. Pulling the plug on the INF Treaty demonstrates once again that ignorance compounded by the drive for domination makes for an extremely dangerous nuclear cocktail.

While the Russian military may indeed have been in breach of the Treaty by testing a new medium-range cruise missile, less well known is that, as Theodore Postol of the Massachusetts Institute of Technology (MIT) has documented, the US Aegis systems deployed in Romania

'have characteristics that make them especially threatening to Russia … If the Aegis-based systems in Eastern Europe were supplied with American cruise missiles—either the existing Tomahawk or a new missile that the United States has been developing—they would become fearsome offensive forces, staged on the frontiers of Russia. And there would be little way for Russia to know whether Aegis systems were loaded with missile defense interceptors or nuclear-armed cruise missiles. The offensive capabilities of the US missile defense installations in Eastern Europe are key to understanding the US-Russia standoff over the INF.'

Of course, the proper response to Russia's cruise missile testing was not to rip up the critically important treaty that functionally ended the Cold War. Instead, it should have prompted intensifying nuclear disarmament diplomacy, as the Russians urged.

Abandoning the Treaty is part-and-parcel of Trump's unilateralist 'America First' vision of US global dominance. Combined with the likely expiration of the New Start Treaty, it will eliminate all nuclear arms agreements between the world's two largest and most dangerous nuclear powers, paving the way for an unrestrained, dangerous and mind-bogglingly costly nuclear arms race.

Withdrawal from the INF Treaty needs to be understood in the context of more than two decades of increasingly aggressive US military policies in relation to Russia: expansion of NATO initiated by the Clinton administration; withdrawal from the Anti-Ballistic Missile (ABM) Treaty by the Bush II-Cheney administration; the Obama administration's commitment to spend $1.2 trillion to develop a new generation of US nuclear weapons and their delivery systems; deployment of missile defences that Moscow fears could be converted into nuclear-armed first strike missiles; and the decision to deploy upgraded and 'more usable' US nuclear weapons to five European NATO countries.

Committed to ensuring that Russia will not be humiliated again as it was in the 1990s, President Putin has reaffirmed his commitment to mutual assured destruction. Russian nuclear-capable missiles are now in Kaliningrad on the northern fringe of Central Europe. In order to evade or overwhelm US missile defences, Russia is deploying a new long-range multiple warhead missile, and hypersonic cruise and other missiles reportedly capable of flying up to five times the speed of sound. Putin has also pledged to deploy a nuclear-powered 'unmanned underwater vehicle' capable of destroying port cities with nuclear weapons.

These new weapons systems mimic and up the ante of the existential threats of the 1980s.

Beyond Trump's and National Security Advisor John Bolton's ostensible concerns about possible Russian Treaty violations, lies their preoccupation with the INF Treaty's limitation on the Pentagon's ability to counter China's military modernization and creation of new island bases in the South China Sea. US withdrawal from the Treaty also needs to be seen in the context of the current struggle for Asia-Pacific – now 'Indo-Pacific' – hegemony. We need to understand withdrawal from the Treaty complements the provocative US South China Sea 'freedom of navigation exercises,' the deployment of US missile defences to Japan and South Korea, and Trump's disastrous trade war initiated with China, all elements of Trump's nationally self-defeating campaign to weaken and contain China.

I'm sorry to say that we likely soon need to be opposing plans to deploy ground-launched cruise missiles to Japan, Taiwan and to a post-Duterte Philippines.

Mikhail Gorbachev was right when he remarked that Trump's announcement of US withdrawal from the INF Treaty was not the work 'of a great mind…With enough political will, any problems of compliance with the existing treaties could be resolved' and, 'there will be no winner in a "war of all against all" – particularly if it ends in a nuclear war'. Though I have no love for Putin, we should appreciate Russia's offer that 'there is still room for dialogue'.

The dangers posed by the collapse of the INF Treaty and likely New START are not abstractions. Both great powers use their nuclear arsenals to dangerously reinforce or expand their imperial spheres of influence. For example, the US threatened possible nuclear attacks on the eves of the 1991 and 2003 Iraq wars and former President Obama repeated 'all options on the table' threats against Iran. It was South Korean President Moon's inspired diplomacy that brought us back from the brink of Trump's 'fire and fury' threat against North Korea. The US has not been alone in practising nuclear brinksmanship. Putin stated that he considered the use of nuclear weapons to ensure Russian control of Crimea, and that he is ready for a 21$^{st}$ century version of the Cuban Missile Crisis. All this adds to the danger of miscalculations and accidents.

I don't think most governments, peace movements or broader civil society appreciate the urgency of this moment. We need to find ways to raise the alarm and bring the great powers back from the brink.

The severity of the crisis is real, and it is being driven by powerful forces in the US, Russia and, differently, in China. It can only be transformed through the development of countervailing political, diplomatic and popular power. I don't claim to know precisely how this can be achieved, but I can point to several possible paths.

The first lies in the US House of Representatives, which has the power of the purse, and the Democratic presidential primary elections. Congressman Adam Smith, Chairman of the House Armed Service Committee, has stated his opposition to funding production and deployment of new nuclear weapons and their delivery systems. Those of us in the US need to do all that we can to stiffen his resolve and to press others in Congress to ensure that there be no money for new nukes and delivery systems. This is possible.

Additionally, the presidential campaign has already begun. Like Representative Smith, Senators Elizabeth Warren and Bernie Sanders have each stated their opposition to the production and deployment of the new nuclear arsenal. They've set a standard that bird doggers in New Hampshire and Iowa, and voters in other states, can press their competitors to match.

There is also the need for mass action here in the US. With the necessary obsession about Trump and his administration's corruptions and assaults on the Constitution, the rule of law, the climate, and just about everything and everyone else except the super-rich, popular mobilization on nuclear or other foreign policy issues remains a challenge. As in the early 1980s, when Europe was the initial bull's-eye for catastrophic nuclear war, if European popular opinion can be mobilized against the new US and Russian nuclear deployments, it can awaken and spur a significant response in the United States. Here we have to look to the incipient European Nuclear Disarmament movement and its allied organizations to bring people onto the streets. Remember the Nuclear Weapons Freeze movement, the local actions it sparked across the country, and our million-strong disarmament rally in 1982 all came in response to European alarms and forced Reagan to negotiate with the Russians.

There is also a role for the Nuclear Weapon Ban Treaty. It can play a role in surrounding and isolating the nuclear powers if those who support the Ban in the Global South and in umbrella states have sufficient will. When the Treaty comes into force, states parties to the Treaty are required to engage and press the nuclear powers to join the Treaty. If those governments are truly serious about creating a nuclear-weapons-free world, they can target sanctions against the nuclear powers' senior officials and nuclear establishments.

And, if umbrella states including NATO members, Japan and Australia are forced by popular movements to sign and ratify the Ban Treaty, or if Jeremy Corbyn comes to power in Britain and signs the Treaty, that would crack the ideological foundations of nuclearism, creating more space and opportunities for forces in the nuclear weapons states to press for meaningful nuclear disarmament

Let me also point to two additional paths away from the new unrestrained arms race. It will cost trillions of dollars, an unimaginable number. But we will see the meaning of those numbers in the funding cuts to social and environmental programmes that are being sacrificed on the altar of nuclearism: access to housing, health care, education, food and much more. This dictates that we must make common cause with forces in our countries struggling for economic, social and environmental justice.

Finally, the nuclear powers tell us that the strategic environment prohibits serious disarmament diplomacy. That environment can be changed, as it was with the Common Security diplomacy of the 1980s. As Georgi Arbatov, who participated in the Palme Commission and greatly influenced Mikhail Gorbachev, wrote, 'we cannot guarantee our own security at the expense of someone else's, but only on the basis of mutual interests'. The common interest then, as now, was 'a commitment to joint survival rather than on a threat of mutual destruction'.

I look forward to seeing where our thinking and actions will take us. Given what we know about the practice of nuclear blackmail, nuclear weapons accidents, miscalculations, and the human costs of the nuclear arms race, 'the hour' to quote my favourite Nobel laureate, 'is getting late'*. Yet we know that another world is possible.


*Bob Dylan, All Along The Watchtower

# Why the INF Treaty Matters

*Katarzyna Kubiak*

*Dr. Kubiak is a Policy Fellow on nuclear and arms control policy at the European Leadership Network. She submitted a paper on 'Consequences for UK Defence of INF Withdrawal' to the Defence Committee of the British House of Commons, which published its controversial report, 'Missile Misdemeanours: Russia and the INF Treaty', in April 2019. She poses some key questions, and makes constructive suggestions, in this updated version.*

**Has the INF Treaty been violated?**

1. The United States and Russia both accuse each other of violating the Intermediate-range Nuclear Forces (INF) Treaty. Each side claims to be in compliance and of providing the relevant data to the other side. Both have failed to offer inspections of their alleged violating systems.

*Alleged Russian violation*

2. In 2014, Washington publicly alleged that Moscow had violated the INF Treaty by testing and, since 2017, deploying a prohibited cruise missile system, designated as the SSC-8 in the United States or 9M729 in Russia.

3. According to the Director of National Intelligence Daniel Coats, Russia flight tested a ground based missile to distances over 500 kilometres from a treaty-compliant launcher (a fixed land-based launcher used for Ship-Launched Cruise Missile (SLCM) tests) and then tested the same missile at ranges below 500 km from a non-compliant launcher (a mobile land-based launcher). By putting the results of the two tests together, Russia is supposed to have developed a missile within the INF Treaty prohibited range that can be launched from a ground-mobile platform, also prohibited.

4. Washington was slow to share the evidence with its European NATO allies. Some European governments viewed the initial US evidence as not compelling or substantial enough. It took Washington more than three years to persuade allies to support its allegations.

5. By the end of November 2018, the Dutch government claimed to have independently confirmed the Russian violation. Yet there is no information specifying the data and methods of analysis. According to *Spiegel Online*, the German intelligence services assessed US evidence (apparently including a satellite video) as 'convincing'.

6. Moscow denies these as 'absolutely groundless [US] accusations'. Russia acknowledged that the 9M729 cruise missile exists, but claims that it has neither been developed nor tested in ranges banned by the INF Treaty and its deployment is in strict compliance with the treaty. According to Deputy Foreign Minister Sergey Ryabkov, a Russian demonstration of the system is not 'justified from either the political or technical perspective'.

7. The limited data that is publicly available does not allow non-state parties to independently evaluate US/NATO allegations. The lack of details on how the Dutch intelligence came to its conclusions, and no public evidence backing *Spiegel Online* information, make it impossible to verify these claims.

8. The US government has been consistent in making the case for a Russian violation. While the diplomatic handling of the assumed Russian violation by the Donald Trump Administration is controversial, it seems plausible to assume that there is merit to US accusations particularly since all NATO allies are firmly behind the US position as demonstrated by the most recent NATO Foreign Ministers statement, issued on 4 December 2018.

9. The Russian government's position might result from a genuine belief of being in compliance and/or from differences in interpreting its activities under the treaty. Russia is in reactive mode, but Moscow has shown interest in a diplomatic solution. The Russian claim that it needs more time to evaluate and respond to US 'information about the dates of the flight tests' could be plausible given the lack of care to due process of the current administration. However, the Russian attempt to include the INF Treaty in a discussion over 'a broader agenda – a whole package of issues of strategic stability and arms control' and politicizing the INF Treaty at the United Nations does not strengthen Moscow's credibility. While Russia is not legally obliged to offer a solution to the United States, failing to make a proactive offer on substantive measures to tackle America's allegations – be it in a mutual basis or alone – calls into question Moscow's good faith

and strengthens the assumption that the Kremlin is not interested in maintaining the treaty.

*Alleged US violation*

10. In response, Moscow accuses the United States of INF Treaty violations on several grounds. It claims that the Mk-41 launchers for the US ground-based ballistic missile defence interceptors deployed in Romania and soon to be deployed in Poland could be used to launch offensive INF Treaty-range Tomahawk cruise missiles. Further, Russia takes the position that US target missiles for ballistic missile defence interceptor tests and US armed drones should be counted under the INF Treaty restrictions.

11. The US State Department claims to have 'repeatedly refuted baseless Russian allegations in detail'. European allies have unconditionally sided with Washington, not pressing the United States on compliance questions.

12. The Russian claims regarding ballistic target missiles and armed UAVs [unmanned aerial vehicle] date 15 and 18 years back, respectively, both have been discussed in the Special Verification Commission and do not raise broader concerns among experts. However, some experts – Western included – acknowledge that there is some substance to the Russian claim regarding the non-compliance potential of the Aegis Ashore Missile Defence System.

13. The US government claims that Aegis Ashore 'lacks the software, fire control hardware, support equipment, and other infrastructure needed to launch offensive ballistic or cruise missiles such as the Tomahawk. (...) Although it utilizes some of the same structural components as the sea-based Mk-41 Vertical Launch System installed on ships, the Aegis Ashore vertical launching system is NOT the same launcher as the sea-based MK-41 Vertical Launch System' [authors note: emphasis original].

14. The 2016 Agreement Between the United States of America and Romania on the Deployment of the United States Ballistic Missile Defence System in Romania only mentions the deployment of US non-nuclear ballistic missile defense interceptors on the territory of Romania. It reconfirms 'the exclusively defensive nature of the United States European Phased Adaptive Approach for Ballistic Missile Defence' and stresses that the facility will 'be used exclusively for self-defence purposes'. The US is

supposed to notify Romania 'of any changes to the interceptors and any permanent change to the facility'.

15. While there is merit to the Russian Aegis Ashore claim, it does not seem plausible that the United States undertook what might seem to be a provocative step to willingly circumvent the INF Treaty. Rather, this is more likely the consequence of a political decision that was badly communicated to Russia and not sufficiently attuned to resolve possible compliance concerns. The US government did not and probably cannot make a convincing case against the Russian accusations of the Aegis Ashore technical specifications. The United States never publicly offered Russia an inspection of the ground-based Mk-41 launcher in order to counter the INF Treaty-related accusations.

### How best could a return to compliance with the Treaty be achieved?

16. Because both parties claim to be in compliance, confirming or repudiating these statements is essential to setting the facts straight.

17. Development of a noncompliant missile carries a different qualitative weight than the deployment of a launcher, yet both are legitimate concerns that should be addressed to the satisfaction of the other party.

18. Providing there is enough political will in Moscow, Washington, and NATO capitals, technical solutions are available. However, concerns can only be resolved on the basis of reciprocity.

19. Both parties should provide comprehensive technical information supporting their allegations.

20. Mutual, on-site inspections and exhibitions of the SSC-8 and the Mk-41 launcher could be an initial step to address the most serious allegations.

21. The United States needs to show that the ground-based 'Aegis Ashore vertical launching system is not the same launcher as the sea-based Mk-41 Vertical Launching System,' that it is indeed 'only capable of launching defensive interceptor missiles,' and that it not only cannot launch Tomahawk missiles but has none of these missiles deployed at the European site. The ongoing upgrade of the Aegis Ashore site in Deveselu and its subsequent offline-setting could serve as a good opportunity to offer Russia a visit.

22. Russia needs to convince the United States that the SSC-8 missile pointed to by Washington does not violate the INF Treaty by showing that it cannot achieve a range between 500 and 5500 km.

23. The lapsed INF Treaty inspection provisions provide a blueprint on how to put respective claims of compliance to the test. Additionally, the New START Treaty Annex on Inspection Activities and the INF Treaty Inspection Protocol provide useful examples for exhibition procedures aimed at demonstrating distinguishing features and confirming the technical characteristics of weapon systems. The Vienna Document with its procedures regarding demonstration of new types of major weapon systems also provides guidelines both sides could follow or adapt.

24. In terms of missile defence test targets and drones, Russia and the United States could work to amend the treaty by rewriting and specifying language where needed.

25. The US ultimatum that Russia has 60 days to 'get rid of' the alleged missile, 'get rid' of the launcher or change the missiles range, and allow for verification does not take into account the Russian perception of its innocence and Russian allegations towards the United States, and thus is deemed to fail.

## What would the consequences be of the US withdrawing from the Treaty?

26. First, the US and NATO lose the legal basis to insist on Russia's return to compliance.

27. Second, it allows Russia to freely field the alleged cruise missile while NATO has neither offensive nor defensive capabilities with which to credibly respond in the short term.

28. Third, the potential willingness of some European governments to capitalize on hosting conventional intermediate-range cruise missiles, should the United States decide to field them, could deepen NATO's divide.

29. Fourth, the demise of the INF Treaty and internal NATO deliberations over an appropriate response could require reopening deliberations on NATO's deterrence and defence posture.

30. Fifth, Ukraine still retains the potential to produce intermediate-range missiles and will no longer have constraints under the treaty, if the agreement ceases.

31. Sixth, the death of the INF Treaty without solving the compliance issue could impede prospects for extending existing arms control agreements, such as the New START Treaty, and negotiating new ones.

32. Finally, the way NATO's nuclear and non-nuclear countries deal with the INF Treaty determines, albeit differently, their trustworthiness, credibility and leadership within the Nuclear Non-Proliferation Treaty (NPT).

### Is the INF Treaty still relevant given the technological and geopolitical developments since it was signed?

33. The INF Treaty remains relevant to global, but especially European security and stability. It is a cornerstone of the current European security order, curbing miscalculation and providing limited escalation stability in Europe. Its collapse would exacerbate the US-Russia and NATO-Russia confrontation. A subsequent arms build-up would be destabilising for Europe, Asia and US-Russian strategic relations.

34. In criticising the INF Treaty, Moscow regularly points to the unrestricted access to intermediate range ground-launched missiles enjoyed by 'almost all countries in the world'. Since the INF Treaty was signed, the horizontal proliferation of intermediate-range missiles has brought the majority of Russian territory within range of a number of countries, including nearly all of its neighbours. In these respects, the 1987 INF treaty is becoming overtaken by events, at least for Russia. In response, Russia has unsuccessfully tried to convince the United States to go for a joint withdrawal from the treaty. On another occasion, Moscow secured Washington's support for the treaty's universalisation, but did not win over the rest of the international community for this idea. Although these attempts remained unsuccessful, Russian decision-makers continued to refrain from withdrawing from the INF Treaty – a right it has under the accord.

35. When threatening US withdrawal from the INF Treaty, President Donald Trump and Secretary of State Michael Pompeo argued that China is not party to the treaty and has intermediate-range weapons that allegedly

put the United States at a disadvantage in the Western Pacific. However, the Chinese INF Treaty-range missiles are not a new technological development that would alter the INF Treaty's legitimacy for the United States. According to Hans M. Kristensen, Director of the Nuclear Information Project at the Federation of American Scientists and an authoritative expert in nuclear weapon systems and programmes, China has had such weapons since 1970. When the INF Treaty was signed, 75% of Chinese nuclear weapons were INF Treaty-range. China has had intermediate-range capability to hit Guam since 1980. The United States never deployed INF-class missiles in the Pacific in response. What has changed since then is that the United States now considers China a 'strategic competitor' and is in the middle of a domestic political debate on the requirement for INF Treaty-range ground-launched missiles in the Pacific.

**What role could the UK play in future discussions of the Treaty?**

36. The deadlock between Russia and United States is not conducive to achieving a constructive bilateral solution. According to the US government, Russia refused discussion of the violating missile at a third bilateral experts meeting on June 21, 2018. Russian Defence Minister Sergei Shoigu is said to have sent US Defense Secretary James Mattis a proposal for launching a dialogue on the INF Treaty in December 2018, but Washington is said to neither having formally acknowledged the receipt of the invitation, nor replied.

37. A future diplomatic initiative to resolve the INF Treaty compliance crisis would need to be initiated by European like-minded states using the small window of opportunity before the US withdrawal comes into effect by August 2nd, 2019. Ideally, the process would be led by a team of professional mediators.

38. The US withdrawal from the INF Treaty will heavily affect European security. Russian concerns relate to the Aegis Ashore in Deveselu, which is part of NATO Ballistic Missile Defence. NATO now supports the US allegations. As such, European NATO allies not only have a valid interest, but also leverage in solving the INF Treaty concerns. So does Belarus, Ukraine and Kazakhstan, which remain active parties to the treaty and participated in the two meetings of the Special Verification Commission which met to discuss questions relating to compliance in 2016 and 2017.

39. The UK government might try to support the German, and win the Dutch and potentially some other European governments to help mediate a solution along the lines of the reciprocal transparency visit concept. European NATO member states should make a case to invite Moscow to an inspection of its Aegis Ashore system, providing that Russia agrees on an inspection of its SSC-8 missile. There are no Aegis Ashore assets in Poland yet, and as such focus should be on the US facility in Romania. While it is highly improbable to envisage the Romanian government at the forefront in offering mutual inspections to Russia, it is also highly improbable for Bucharest to be willing to take the blame for letting a critical arms control treaty die.

40. If Washington proceeds with the withdrawal, a European pledge to refrain from deploying INF Treaty-class missiles, provided Russia does not deploy more of them and reverses existing deployments, would be one option to mitigate an unnecessary and costly arms spiral.

41. If Moscow proceeds with further deployments, European NATO member states should seek options aimed at risk reduction. This could include a verifiable quantitative limit on such missiles to a few systems on both sides of the NATO-Russia border and/or a verifiable qualitative ban on arming such systems with nuclear warheads. Such an effort should not be seen as a reward for bad behaviour. Rather, it should be recognized as an investment in preventing an arms race, as a step to realize the European commitment to nuclear non-proliferation and disarmament, and as a way for Europe to remain central in shaping the global nuclear weapons landscape. As with the Iran nuclear accord, Europe has a major role to play and a major stake in the outcome.

42. London could also support Berlin in generating proposals for and implementing a regime that creates new and/or enhances existing transparency and other sets of rules for missiles and missile technology.

*Detailed references available online at*:
http://data.parliament.uk/writtenevidence/committeeevidence.svc/evidenc edocument/defence-committee/consequences-for-uk-defence-of-inf-withdrawal/written/94773.html

# European Nuclear Disarmament
## A New Statement

President Trump's threat that the United States will withdraw from the Intermediate-Range Nuclear Forces (INF) Treaty undermines peace and security in Europe, as the European Union has quickly made clear.

The INF Treaty, signed by Presidents Gorbachev and Reagan in 1987, bans all ground-based missiles – nuclear and conventional – with ranges between 500 and 5500km. It addresses the risk of 'limited' nuclear war, which sparked a Europe-wide movement of opposition and in favour of a nuclear-weapons-free zone in Europe, as expressed in the European Nuclear Disarmament (END) Appeal of 1980.

The END Appeal specifically sought the removal of medium range mobile nuclear weapons, deployed on Soviet territory and by the United States at bases in six European NATO member countries, in order to save the continent from becoming a nuclear battleground. It warned 'we are entering the most dangerous decade in human history'. Appallingly, danger intensifies again. In January, the Bulletin of the Atomic Scientists moved forward the hands of the 'Doomsday Clock' to two minutes to midnight. As the year draws to a close, President Trump's announcement drives the world nearer to the nuclear precipice.

We call on everyone concerned with peace and security to join in raising the alarm over the likely consequences of scrapping the INF Treaty and to work towards the creation of more Nuclear-Weapons-Free-Zones, including in Europe. These efforts will complement existing global disarmament initiatives, including the Treaty on the Prohibition of Nuclear Weapons, recently agreed at the United Nations.

**To support the statement and the work of European Nuclear Disarmament, sign up here:** https://forms.gle/DccRQfcBvQp77Gdi9

# STEPHEN F. COHEN

# WAR WITH RUSSIA?

## FROM PUTIN & UKRAINE TO TRUMP & RUSSIAGATE

# War with Russia?

*Stephen F. Cohen*

*The author is Professor Emeritus of Politics at Princeton University and Professor Emeritus of Russian Studies and History at New York University. His contacts with the Russell Foundation go back to the 1970s and the successful campaign to rehabilitate Nikolai Bukharin in the Soviet Union, when Professor Cohen's classic political biography,* Bukharin and the Bolshevik Revolution, *was published. Professor Cohen has consistently sought to uphold* détente *between Russia and the United States. We are grateful to him and his publishers for permission to reprint the Afterword from his cautionary and timely new book,* War With Russia? *(Hot Books, an imprint of Skyhorse Publishing, New York)*

> *'The Owl of Minerva spreads its wings only with the falling of dusk.'*
>
> Hegel

*War With Russia?,* like a biography of a living person, is a book without an end. The title is a warning – akin to what the late Gore Vidal termed "a journalistic alert-system"[1] – not a prediction. Hence the question mark. I cannot foresee the future. The book's overarching theme is informed by past and current facts, not by any political agenda, ideological commitment, or magical prescience.

To restate that theme: The new US-Russian Cold War is more dangerous than was its 40-year predecessor, which the world survived. The chances are even greater, as I hope readers already understand, that this one could result, inadvertently or intentionally, in actual war between the two nuclear superpowers. Herein lies another ominous indication. During the preceding Cold War, the possibility of nuclear catastrophe was in the forefront of American mainstream political and media discussion, and of policy-making. During the new one, it rarely seems to be even a concern.

As I finish War *With Russia?,* the facts and mounting crises they document grow worse, especially in the US political-media establishment where, as readers also understand, I think the new Cold War originated and has been repeatedly escalated. Consider finally a few examples from the latter months of 2018, some of them not unlike political and media developments during the run-up to the US war in Iraq or, historians have told us, when the great powers "sleepwalked" into World War I:

• Russiagate's core allegations, none of them yet proven, had become a central part of the new Cold War. If nothing else, they severely constrained President Trump's capacity to conduct crisis-negotiations with Moscow while they further vilified Russian President Putin for having, it was widely asserted, personally ordered "an attack on America" during the 2016 presidential campaign. Hollywood liberals, it will be recalled, quickly omitted the question mark, declaring, "We are at war." In October 2018, the would-be titular head of the Democratic Party, Hillary Clinton, added her voice to this reckless allegation, flatly stating that the United States was "attacked by a foreign power" and equating it with "the September 11, 2001, terrorist attacks."[2]

Clinton may have been prompted by another outburst of *New York Times* and *Washington Post* malpractice. On September 20 and 23 respectively, those exceptionally influential papers devoted thousands of words, illustrated with sinister prosecutorial graphics, to special retellings of the Russiagate narrative they had assiduously promoted for nearly two years, along with the narrative's serial fallacies, selective and questionable history, and factual errors. (In the front of its issue, the *Times* reporters explained that "the goal of the project ... was to bring people back to a story they might have abandoned.")

Again, for example, the now-infamous Paul Manafort was said to have been "pro-Kremlin" during the period at issue when in fact he was pro-European Union. Again, the disgraced General Michael Flynn was accused of "troubling" contacts when he did nothing wrong or unprecedented in having conversations with a Kremlin representative on behalf of President elect Trump. Again, the two papers criminalized the idea that "the United States and Russia should look for areas of mutual interest," once the premise of *détente*. And again, the *Times*, while assuring readers its "Special Report" was "what we now know with certainty," buried the nullifying acknowledgment deep in its some 10,000 words: "No public evidence has emerged showing that [Trump's] campaign conspired with Russia." (The white-collar criminal indictments and guilty pleas cited were so unrelated they again added up to Russiagate without Russia.)

Astonishingly, neither paper gave any credence to an emphatic statement by Bob Woodward – normally considered the most authoritative chronicler of Washington's political secrets – that after two years of research he had found "no evidence of collusion" between Trump and Russia. Endorsing the *Post* version, a prominent historian even assured his readers that the widely discredited anti-Trump Steele dossier – the source of so many allegations – was "increasingly plausible."[3, 4]

Nor were the *Times*, *Post*, and other print media alone in these practices, which continued to slur dissenting opinions. CNN's leading purveyor of

Russiagate allegations tweeted that an American third-party presidential candidate had been "repeating Russian talking points on its interference in the 2016 election and on US foreign policy."[5] Another prominent CNN figure was, so to speak, more geopolitical, warning, "Only a fool takes Vladimir Putin at his word in Syria," thereby ruling out US-Russian cooperation in that war-torn country.[6] Much the same continued almost nightly on MSNBC.

For most mainstream media outlets, Russiagate had become, it seemed, a kind of cult journalism that no counter-evidence or analysis could dent – though I try in this book – and thus itself increasingly a major contributing factor to the new Cold War. Still more, what began two years earlier as complaints about Russian "meddling" in the US presidential election became by October 2018, for the *New Yorker*[7] and other publications, including the *Times* and the *Post*, an accusation that the Kremlin had actually put Donald Trump in the White House. For this seditious charge, there was also no convincing evidence – nor any precedent in American history.

• At a higher level, by fall 2018, current and former US officials were making nearly unprecedented threats against Moscow. The ambassador to NATO threatened to "take out" any Russian missiles she thought violated a 1987 treaty, a step that would certainly risk nuclear war.[8] The Secretary of the Interior threatened a "naval blockade" of Russia.[9] In yet another Russophobic outburst, the soon-to-retire ambassador to the UN, Nikki Haley, declared that "lying, cheating and rogue behaviour" are a "norm of Russian culture."[10]

These may have been outlandish statements by untutored political appointees, though they inescapably again raised the question: who was making Russia policy in Washington – President Trump with his avowed policy of "cooperation" or someone else?

But how to explain, other than as unbridled extremism, comments by a former US ambassador to Moscow, himself a longtime professor of Russian politics and favoured mainstream commentator? According to him, Russia had become a "rogue state," its policies "criminal actions," and the "world's worst threat." It had to be countered by "preemptive sanctions that would go into effect automatically" – "every day," if deemed necessary.[11] Considering "crushing" sanctions then being prepared by a bipartisan group of US senators "to punish" Moscow[12], this would be nothing less than a declaration of permanent war against Russia: economic war, but war nonetheless.

• Meanwhile, other new Cold War fronts were becoming more fraught with hot war, none more so than Syria. On September 15, 2018, Syrian missiles accidentally shot down an allied Russian surveillance aircraft, killing all fifteen crew members. The cause was combat subterfuge by Israeli warplanes in the area. The reaction in Moscow was indicative – and potentially ominous.

At first, Putin, who had developed good relations with Israel's political leadership, said the incident was an accident caused by the fog of war. His own Defence Ministry, however, loudly protested that Israel was responsible. Putin quickly retreated to a more hardline position, and in the end vowed to send to Syria Russia's highly effective S-300 surface-to-air defence system, a prize long sought by both Syria and Iran.

Clearly, Putin was not the ever "aggressive Kremlin autocrat" unrelentingly portrayed by US mainstream media. Still a moderate in the Russian context, he again made a major decision by balancing conflicting groups and interests. In this instance, he accommodated longstanding hardliners ("hawks") in his own security establishment.

The result was yet another Cold War tripwire. With the S-300s installed in Syria, Putin could in effect impose a "no-fly-zone" over large areas of the country, which had been ravaged by war due, in no small part, to the combat presence of several foreign powers. (Russia and Iran were there legally; the United States and Israel were not.) If so, it meant a new "red line" that Washington and its ally Israel would have to decide whether or not to cross. Considering the mania in Washington and in the mainstream media, it was hard to be confident restraint would prevail.

All this unfolded around the third anniversary of Russia's military intervention in Syria in September 2015. At that time, Washington pundits denounced Putin's "adventure" and were sure it would fail. Three years later, "Putin's Kremlin" had destroyed the vicious Islamic State's grip on significant parts of Syria, for which it still got no credit in Washington; all but restored President Assad's control over most of the country; and made itself the ultimate arbiter of Syria's future. In keeping with his Russia policy, President Trump probably was inclined to join Moscow's peace process, though it was unlikely the mostly Democratic Russiagate party would permit him to do so. (For perspective, recall that, in 2016, presidential candidate Hillary Clinton called for a US no-fly zone over Syria to defy Russia.)

• As I finish this book, another Cold War front also became more fraught. The US-Russian proxy war in Ukraine acquired a new dimension. In addition to the civil war in Donbass, Moscow and Kiev began challenging the other's ships in the Sea of Azov, near the vital Ukrainian port of Mariupol. Trump was being pressured to supply Kiev with naval and other weapons to wage this evolving maritime war, yet another potential tripwire. Here too the president should instead have put his administration's weight behind the long-stalled Minsk peace accords. But that approach also seemed ruled out by Russiagate, which by October 2018 included yet another *Times* columnist, Frank Bruni, branding all such initiatives by Trump "pimping for Putin."[13]

After five years of extremism exemplified by these more recent examples of risking war with Russia, there remained, for the first time in decades of Cold War history, no countervailing forces in Washington – no pro-*détente* wing of the Democratic or Republican Party, no influential anti-Cold War opposition anywhere, no real public debate. There was only Trump, with all the loathing he inspired, and even he had not reminded the nation or his own party that the presidents who initiated major episodes of *détente* in the 20th century were also Republicans-Eisenhower, Nixon, Reagan. This too seemed to be an inadmissible "alternative fact."

And so the eternal question, not only for Russians: what is to be done? There was a ray of light, though scarcely more. In August 2018, Gallup asked Americans what kind of policy toward Russia they favoured. Even amid the torrent of vilifying Russiagate allegations and Russophobia, 58 per cent wanted "to improve relations with Russia" as opposed to 36 per cent preferring "strong diplomatic and economic steps against Russia."[14]

This reminds us that the new Cold War, from NATO's eastward expansion and the Ukrainian crisis to Russiagate, has been an elite project. Why, after the end of the Soviet Union in 1991, US elites ultimately chose Cold War rather than partnership with Russia is a question beyond the limits of this book and perhaps my ability to answer. As for the role of US intelligence elites, what I have termed Intelgate, efforts are still under way to disclose it fully, and being thwarted.[15]

A full explanation of the Cold War choice would include the political-media establishment's needs – ideological, foreign-policy, budgetary, among others – for an "enemy."[16] Or, Cold War having prevailed for more than half of US-Russian relations during the century since 1917, maybe it was habitual. Substantial "meddling" in the 2016 election by Ukraine and Israel, to illustrate the point, did not become a political scandal.[17] In any event, once this approach to post-Soviet Russia began, promoting it was not hard. The legendary humorist Will Rogers quipped back in the 1930s, "Russia is a country that no matter what you say about it, it's true." Back then, before the 40-year Cold War and nuclear weapons, the quip was funny, but no longer.

Whatever the full explanation, many of the consequences I have analyzed along the way continue to unfold, not a few unintended and unfavourable to America's real national interests. Russia's turn away from the West, its "pivot to China," is now widely acknowledged and embraced by many Moscow policy thinkers.[18] Even European allies occasionally stand with Moscow against Washington.[19] The US-backed Kiev government still covers up who was really behind the 2014 Maidan "snipers' massacre" that brought it to power.[20] Mindless US sanctions have helped Putin to repatriate oligarchic assets abroad, an estimated $90 billion already in 2018.[21] Mainstream media persist in distorting Putin's foreign polices into something "that even the Soviet Union never dared to try."[22] And when an anonymous White House "insider" exposed in the *Times* "the president's amorality," the only actual policy he or she singled out was Russia policy.[23]

I have focused enough on the surreal demonizing of Putin – the *Post* even managed to characterize popular support for his substantial contribution to improving life in Moscow as "a deal with the devil" – but it is important to note that this "derangement" is far from world-wide.[24] Even a *Post* correspondent conceded that "the Putin brand has captivated anti-establishment and anti-American politicians all over the world."[25] A worldly British journalist confirmed that as a result "many countries in the world now look for a reinsurance policy with Russia."[26] And an American journalist living in Moscow reported that "ceaseless demonization of Putin personally has in fact sanctified him, turned him into the Patron Saint of Russia."[27]

Again, in light of all this, what can be done? Sentimentally, and with some historical precedents, we of democratic beliefs traditionally look to "the people," to voters, to bring about change. But foreign policy has long been the special prerogative of elites. In order to change Cold War policy fundamentally, leaders are needed. When the times beckon, they may emerge out of established, even deeply conservative, elites, as did unexpectedly Ronald Reagan and Mikhail Gorbachev in the mid-1980s. But given the looming danger of war with Russia, is there time? Is any leader visible on the American political landscape who will say to his or her elite and party, as Gorbachev did, "If not now, when? If not us, who?"

We also know that such leaders, though embedded in and insulated by their elites, hear and read other, non-conformist voices, other thinking. The once-venerated American journalist Walter Lippmann observed, "When all think alike, no one is thinking." This book is my modest attempt to inspire more thinking.

## NOTES

1. Victor Navasky and Katrina vanden Heuvel, eds., *The Best of The Nation*, New York, 2000, p. xvii
2. Reported by Felicia Sonmez, *washingtonpost.com*, October 2, 2018
3. Woodward, realclearpolitics, September 14, 2018
4. Kai Bird, *The Washington Post,* September 30 2018
5. Jim Sciutto, Tweet, May 1, 2018
6. Nie Robertson, CNN.com, September 18, 2018
7. Jane Mayer, October 1, 2018, pp. 18-26
8. Kay Bailey Hutchison quoted by businessinsider.com, October 2
9. southfront.org, September 30
10. Michael Schwirtz, *nytimes.com*, September 17
11. Michael McFaul, *washingtonpost.com*, September 28, 2018
12. *Washington Post* editorial, September 9
13. *New York Times,* October 7
14. news.gallup.com/polV24 1 1 24
15. On September 22, 2018, the *Times* reported that Deputy Attorney General Rod Rosenstein had proposed secretly recording President Trump. Rosenstein denied the report, but the *Times* did not retract its story. On the same day, the *Times* also reported that intelligence agencies had dissuaded the president from declassifying documents directly related to Intelgate.
16. Two leading geopolitical thinkers have presented at least partial explanations. See John Mearsheimer, *Foreign Affairs,* September/October 2014; and Anatol Lieven, *Survival,* Vol. 60, issue 5, 2018
17. See, e.g., Kenneth P. Vogel and David Stern, *politico.com,* January 11, 2017; and Aaron Mate, *TheNation.com,* December 5, 2017
18. Sergei Karaganov, *Johnson's Russia List*, September 24, 2018
19. Andrew Rettman, euobserver.com, September 26, 2018
20. Ivan Katchanovski, *Johnson's Russia* List, September 17, 2018
21. Tyler Durden, ibid., September 24, 2018
22. Jackson Diehl, *Washington Post,* March 19, 2018
23. *New York Times* opinion page, September 6, 2018
24. Anton Troianovski, *Washington Post,* September 9, 2018
25. Anton Troianovski, *washingtonpost.com,* July 12, 2018
26. Patrick Cockburn, *Johnson's Russia List*, September 24, 2018
27. Jeffrey Tayler, *theatlantic.com,* March 18, 2018

## NATO member countries

Twenty-nine members contribute to promoting security and stability through diplomatic, political and military means. They are committed to the principle of collective defence, which means that an attack against one member or more is considered as an attack against all. NATO also develops partnerships with non-NATO countries and is involved in crisis management operations and missions.

ICELAND
  Reykjavik

NORWAY

Oslo

CANADA

UNITED KINGDOM    DENMARK

NETHERLANDS
BELGIUM

Bert

IRELAND
    Dublin

Amsterdam

GERMANY

London

Brussels

LUXEMBOURG

Luxembourg

Ottawa

UNITED STATES

Paris

FRANCE

Washington D.C.

SWITZERLAND
SLOVENIA
CROATIA
SERBIA
MONTENEGRO

Bern

ITA

PORTUGAL

SPAIN

MAL

Madrid

Lisbon

Tunis

Algiers

H

## Mediterranean Dialogue countries

These countries participate in a security dialogue with NATO to improve mutual understanding and contribute towards regional security through stronger practical cooperation. At present, there are seven participating countries, which can consult collectively and individually with NATO.

Rabat

MOROCCO

TUNISIA

ALGERIA

## Istanbul C
## Initiative

This initiative offers practical bilateral sec contribute to global have joined.

MAURITANIA
  Nouakchott

[1] The State of Israel has designated Jerusalem as its capital. The position of the United Nations on the question of Jerusalem is contained in several Resolutions of the General Assembly and the Security Council concerning this question.

The boundaries and names shown and the designatio

## Euro-Atlantic Partners

Partnership with non-NATO countries started as early as 1991 to help often newly independent states build a solid democratic environment, maintain political stability and modernise armed forces. Discussions on security issues of common interest take place within a multilateral forum called the Euro-Atlantic Partnership Council and practical cooperation is organised with individual partner countries through NATO's Partnership for Peace programme.

## Partners across the globe

NATO has developed bilateral relations with a number of countries which are not part of NATO's other partnership frameworks. They include countries such as Australia, Colombia, Japan, the Republic of Korea, New Zealand, Pakistan, Iraq, Afghanistan and Mongolia. They develop cooperation with NATO in areas of mutual interest and some contribute actively to NATO operations either militarily or in some other way.

FINLAND
Helsinki
ESTONIA
Tallinn
Riga
LATVIA
LITHUANIA
Vilnius
Warsaw
AND
BELARUS
Minsk
LIC
Kyiv
VAKIA
NGARY
udapest
ROMANIA
Chisinau
Bucharest
Belgrade
BULGARIA
Padgorica
Sofia
REP. OF MOLDOVA
Skopje
Tirana
GEORGIA
Tbilisi
Athens
Ankara
Yerevan
Baku
GREECE
TURKEY
AZERBAIJAN
IA
ISRAEL
JORDAN
ARMENIA
ONIA
Amman
Cairo
EGYPT
KUWAIT
BAHRAIN
QATAR
Kuwait City
Manama
Doha
Abu Dhabi
UNITED ARAB EMIRATES

RUSSIA
Moscow
KAZAKHSTAN
Astana
UZBEKISTAN
Tashkent
Bishkek
KYRGYZ REP.
TURKMENISTAN
Ashgabat
Dushanbe
TAJIKISTAN

UKRAINE

ion
s

der Middle East region
th NATO so as to
. To date, four countries

www.nato.int

# Russian Pillar

*Vladimir Chizhov*

*In March 2019, the Permanent Representative of the Russian Federation to the European Union, Ambassador Vladimir Chizhov, emphasised our common Eurasian home when he addressed the Delphi Economic Forum in Greece. He sketches the broad outlines of Russia's view of the current international order.*

I would suggest that we start from the beginning and try to contemplate what the international world order is *per se*. For centuries the world lived within Westphalian sovereignty, then the First World War brought us the system of Versailles and, in 1945 in the Russian city of Yalta, countries of the anti-Hitler coalition agreed on how they would co-exist taking into account the results of the Second World War. However, those agreements were soon swept away by the waves of a new confrontation, namely the Cold War.

But the moment came when the Cold War, with its concept of mutual assured destruction, was gone too. What then replaced it? Alas, while a part of our Eurasian continent was going through painful political and economic transformations in pursuit of an optimal democratic organisation and a fair market model that would suit it most, the so-called 'enlightened' West, professing its alleged experience and wisdom, proclaimed 'the end of history' and defined the triumph of an arbitrary set of liberal values and globalisation as the world development vector with no alternative, as a new formula of the 'bright future for all mankind'.

However, failure awaited the authors of social, economic and political engineering at this turn as well. The basically objective globalisation process did not follow the path they had marked. It became obvious that other continents and centres of power, rather than the traditional West, were starting to play a key role. Thereby, the world entered an era of multi-polarity.

It is not a coincidence that at the current stage we witness the widest ever plurality of opinions on what the international world order is and, more importantly, what it should be. It is common knowledge that the modern system of international law was formed within the institutions that had been established following the Second World War, first of all the United Nations, but also the European Union, the Council of Europe, the Organisation for Security and Co-operation in Europe and, no matter how paradoxical it may sound, NATO. (The latter, I would note, continuing to spasmodically enlarge rather out of necessity than choice.) However, today the very notion of 'international law' is subject to revision and dilution. For a number of years now our European and American partners, instead of adhering to this well-known and clear-cut term, have been implanting in their vocabulary and official documents the formula 'internationally recognised rules and norms'. Moreover, they are trying to accustom their interlocutors around the world to it. Meanwhile, inventors of this novelty find it difficult to explain what the difference between law and these 'rules and norms' is, and who had actually recognised the latter and when.

It is natural that Russia, being a responsible international player, a nuclear power, and Permanent Member of the UN Security Council, should be concerned with this situation. We have felt this threat long enough and as, I would repeat, a responsible power, have generated quite a few far-reaching initiatives throughout the last two decades that are aimed at strengthening the world order on the basis of international law and establishing such a security system, first and foremost in Europe, that would provide equal guarantees to all. Besides, Russia has never tried to monopolise this work, and was always open to co-operation with those who were ready to take part in it.

Neither did we refuse initiatives suggested by others. For instance, when in 2010 NATO published its Strategic Concept we positively assessed well-formulated principles of 'security guarantees' and suggested extending them to all countries of Europe. The answer we got was: our proposal is for Alliance members only, so please be content with second class security. It is clear that, with such an approach, talking about equal distribution of security guarantees over Eurasian space was pointless.

Against this background some European countries opted for a simplified way – gave up and rushed to join NATO without thinking that the day would come when they would be requested to incur unbearable and unjustified expenses, participate in missions and operations far from their borders and interests, as well as deploy foreign military bases on their territories. And the Russian proposal to sign a European Security Treaty that would have provided for making legally binding the well-known principle that no one shall enhance one's security at the expense of security of others (enshrined, by the way, as a political commitment in the OSCE

Charter for European Security signed by 54 Heads of State and Government) remained unaddressed.

However, even under such circumstances we do not give up and continue upholding the above-mentioned principles. Meanwhile, given particular aspects of Russian mentality, political culture and perhaps the old-fashioned, as it may seem to many, concept of decency, Moscow never imposes anything on anyone, and does not interfere in internal affairs of other states – contrary to statements certain capitals consider it possible to make following the fashion of blaming 'omnipotent' Russia for all the troubles in the world.

At the same time, some of our 'prosecutors' feel free to impose on other countries their own views on how the latter should live in such a cynical manner that can be described as absolute disregard for all norms of inter-state behaviour. One does not need to go far to find examples: right now we are witnessing Washington's unprecedented interference in the domestic affairs of Venezuela. The US openly calls on the military of the country to defect to a self-proclaimed political leader and threatens with persecution those who remain faithful to their oath. Genuine economic terror is unleashed, sinister extra-territorial sanctions are introduced. Washington managed to 'wear down' EU Member States – except, I would particularly stress, Greece, Cyprus, Slovakia and Italy, as well as the Vatican – resulting in the fact that the 'International Contact Group' formed by the European Union took a biased stance, and thereby deprived itself of the opportunity to act as an impartial mediator.

The situation around Venezuela is obviously a manifestation of a consistent systemic line to ruin the current architecture of world legal order, rather than a solitary case or unremarkable episode. Planting across the information sphere unsupported accusations against certain countries of carrying out hideous chemical attacks and immediately, without any judicial proceedings, imposing sanctions or even launching air strikes are considered to be almost the norm today. It is particularly alarming that this line is also adopted in the military sphere, in non-proliferation of nuclear weapons. We have to acknowledge that today's situation is in a way much more dangerous than the one of the Cold War years – then, for all the depth of ideological differences, common sense and responsibility for the world's fate pushed antagonistic powers to take wise decisions in the area of arms control and disarmament.

Today, we are virtually on the edge of the last line. Its crossing will mean complete dismantling of checks and balances in the nuclear field. And it is not about passions or whims of particular leaders, it is rather about a consistent policy that was formed 17 years ago, at the time of another US Administration – the one that derailed the Anti-Ballistic Missile Treaty. And each time Washington denounced another treaty with Russia it was done under an absolutely invented pretext. As a result the New START Treaty is, in fact, the only one left, its lifespan stretching only until 5 February 2021.

A similar situation is observed in the field of economy. It is worth noting that the system of pipelines ensuring European energy security was created when the Cold War was at its height. In those days there existed, of course, forces that tried to hinder the development of these projects, but the then leaders of countries of Western Europe managed to find the strength not to submit to this pressure. We can only hope that the current generation of European leaders will inherit their courage.

Speaking about economy I need to emphasise that attempts to influence Russia's policy via sanctions are ridiculous. Events of recent years demonstrated that such efforts are in vain and, by the way, make the interests of European business also suffer a lot, as well as our relations in general, including with our largest trade and economic partner – the European Union.

Against this backdrop the easiest thing for Russia would be to follow a trend that is in fashion today and 'pivot to Asia', especially since it is there that the bigger part of my country's territory lies. Actually, we are increasingly active in developing mutually beneficial co-operation with the People's Republic of China, ASEAN countries [Association of Southeast Asian Nations], and other Asian partners, but we are not doing it to undermine or punish Europe. We do not make friends 'against Europe' or the West as a whole. Figuratively speaking, we are implementing the concept projected by the Russian coat of arms whose double-headed eagle (though admittedly inherited from our common ancestral homeland with Greece, Byzantium) looks at the same time to the West and to the East. I would add that Russia, as a country located on two continents and thereby uniting Eurasia by virtue of its geography, history and cultural tradition, is genuinely interested in maintaining equally friendly relations on the West and on the East.

Currently, leaders of major EU countries are more and more often thinking of a new configuration of co-operation in Europe and are more outspoken about the need to take their fate in their hands. I believe it is important that EU Member States remember that they will not be able to uphold their positions against rising economic giants – in Asia today, in Latin America tomorrow, in Africa the day after tomorrow – unless they listen closely to Russia's words about establishing a common economic and humanitarian space in Eurasia. Defending what we call 'European civilisation' is only possible if one of its supporting pillars, Russia, is fully engaged.

Meanwhile, the world is witnessing a deficit of mutual responsibility of nation states, including those the UN Charter assigns with special responsibility for maintaining global peace and security. Aspiring in no way to the laurels of the Oracle of Delphi, I would nevertheless take the courage to predict: unless Russia's partners in the UN Security Council shoulder this responsibility, a 'legal jungle' will emerge on our planet faster than we may assume. In my view, it would be an extremely lamentable outcome of reflecting on the heritage of the first democrats in the history of mankind, those who lived in Ancient Greece and, I am sure, put much brighter hopes on their descendants.

NATO Aegis Ashore Ballistic Missile Defence, Deveselu, Romania

# 'Missile Misdemeanours'

*Russian Embassy Press Officer's reply to a media question concerning the Report of the House of Commons Defence Committee 'Missile Misdemeanours: Russia and the INF Treaty'*

**Question**: How could you comment on the Report of the House of Commons Defence Committee, which blames Russia for the collapse of the Intermediate-Range Nuclear Forces (INF) Treaty?

**Answer**: We have carefully studied the report of British parliamentarians and, in our opinion, it distorts the true state of affairs surrounding the INF Treaty and contains one-sided assessments. Russia strongly rejects baseless allegations of non-compliance with the INF Treaty. The responsibility for the collapse of the Treaty rests entirely with the United States. It was Washington that deliberately brought the situation to a deadlock and rejected our proposal to settle reciprocal claims on the basis of mutual transparency.

Willing to preserve the INF Treaty, we have repeatedly expressed our concern over non-compliance by Washington. As the US media have recently reported with reference to Pentagon representatives, the United States plans to conduct a medium-range ground-based missile test in August [2019], and a ballistic one in November. Obviously it is impossible to establish production of such weapons and prepare for tests so quickly, in just a few months. Therefore, the relevant work has been conducted by the Americans for a while, under the ban.

It is precisely the question that we have been consistently raising: under the guise of using target missiles to test missile defence systems, the US was working on the medium-range ground-based ballistic missile technology. We have been pointing out that, since 2015, the US has deployed launchers capable to launch medium-range cruise missiles from the ground in the missile defence base in Romania. The same launchers are to appear in 2020 on the site constructed by Americans in Poland.

Unfortunately, British parliamentarians have preferred to ignore these and other well-known facts in their report.

*17 April 2019*

# 'Yes' for an answer

*Lawrence Wittner*

*Dr. Wittner is Professor of History Emeritus at SUNY/Albany and author of* Confronting the Bomb *(Stanford University Press)*

At the beginning of February 2019, the two leading nuclear powers took an official step toward resumption of the nuclear arms race. On February 1, the US government, charging Russian violations of the Intermediate-range Nuclear Forces (INF) Treaty, announced that it would pull out of the agreement and develop new intermediate-range missiles banned by it. The following day, Russian President Vladimir Putin suspended his government's observance of the treaty, claiming that this was done as a "symmetrical" response to the US action and that Russia would develop nuclear weapons outlawed by the agreement.

In this fashion, the 1987 Soviet-American INF Treaty – which had eliminated thousands of destabilizing nuclear weapons, set the course for future nuclear disarmament agreements between the two nuclear superpowers, and paved the way for an end to the Cold War – was formally dispensed with.

Actually, the scrapping of the treaty should not have come as a surprise. After all, the rulers of nations, especially "the great powers," are rarely interested in limiting their access to powerful weapons of war, including nuclear weapons. Indeed, they usually favour weapons buildups by their own nation and, thus, end up in immensely dangerous and expensive arms races with other nations.

Donald Trump exemplifies this embrace of nuclear weapons. During his presidential campaign, he made the bizarre claim that the 7,000-weapon US nuclear arsenal "doesn't work," and promised to restore it to its full glory. Shortly after his election, Trump tweeted: "The United States must greatly strengthen and expand its nuclear capability." The following day, with his customary insouciance, he remarked simply: "Let it be an arms race."

Naturally, as president, he has been a keen supporter of a $1.7 trillion refurbishment of the entire US nuclear weapons complex, including the building of new nuclear weapons. Nor has he hesitated to brag about U.S. nuclear prowess. In connection with his war of words with North Korean leader Kim Jong-un, Trump boasted: "I too have a Nuclear Button, but it is a much bigger and more powerful one than his."

Russian leaders, too, though not as overtly provocative, have been impatient to build new nuclear weapons. As early as 2007, Putin complained to top-level US officials that only Russia and the United States were covered by the INF Treaty; therefore, unless other nations were brought into the agreement, "it will be difficult for us to keep within the [treaty] framework." The following year, Sergey Ivanov, the Russian defence minister, publicly bemoaned the INF agreement, observing that intermediate-range nuclear weapons "would be quite useful for us" against China.

By 2014, according to the US government and arms control experts, Russia was pursuing a cruise missile programme that violated the INF agreement, although Putin denied that the missile was banned by the treaty and claimed, instead, that the US missile defense system was out of compliance. And so the offending missile programme continued, as did Russian programmes for blood-curdling types of nuclear weapons outside the treaty's framework. In 2016, Putin criticized "the naïve former Russian leadership" for signing the INF Treaty in the first place. When the US government pulled out of the treaty, Putin not only quickly proclaimed Russia's withdrawal, but announced plans for building new nuclear weapons and said that Russia would no longer initiate nuclear arms control talks with the United States.

The leaders of the seven other nuclear-armed nations have displayed much the same attitude. All have recently been upgrading their nuclear arsenals, with China, India, Pakistan, and North Korea developing nuclear weapons that would be banned by the INF Treaty. Efforts by the US government, in 2008, to bring some of these nations into the treaty were rebuffed by their governments. In the context of the recent breakdown of the INF Treaty, China's government (which, among them, possesses the largest number of such weapons) has praised the agreement for carrying forward the nuclear disarmament process and improving international relations, but has opposed making the treaty a multilateral one – a polite way of saying that nuclear disarmament should be confined to the Americans and the Russians.

Characteristically, all the nuclear powers have rejected the 2017 UN treaty prohibiting nuclear weapons. But the history of the INF Treaty's emergence provides a more heartening perspective.

During the late 1970s and early 1980s, in response to the advent of government officials championing a nuclear weapons buildup and talking glibly of nuclear war, an immense surge of popular protest swept around the world. Antinuclear demonstrations of unprecedented size convulsed Western Europe, Asia, and North America. Even within Communist nations, protesters defied authorities and took to the streets. With opinion polls showing massive opposition to the deployment of new nuclear weapons and the waging of nuclear war, mainstream organizations and political parties sharply condemned the nuclear buildup and called for nuclear disarmament.

Consequently, hawkish government officials began to reassess their priorities. In the fall of 1983, with some five million people busy protesting the US plan to install intermediate-range nuclear weapons in Western Europe, Ronald Reagan told his secretary of state: "If things get hotter and hotter and arms control remains an issue, maybe I should . . . propose eliminating all nuclear weapons." Previously, to dampen antinuclear protest, Reagan and other NATO hawks had proposed the "zero option" – scrapping plans for US missile deployment in Western Europe for Soviet withdrawal of INF missiles from Eastern Europe. But Russian leaders scorned this public relations gesture until Mikhail Gorbachev, riding the wave of popular protest, decided to call Reagan's bluff. As a result, recalled a top administration official, "we had to take yes for an answer." In 1987, amid great popular celebration, Reagan and Gorbachev signed the INF Treaty.

Although the rulers of nuclear-armed nations are usually eager to foster nuclear buildups, substantial public pressure can secure their acceptance of nuclear disarmament.

# Force for good?

## *How to respond to the new nuclear deterrence and disarmament crisis*

*Commander Robert Green RN (Ret'd)*

*A former operator of British nuclear weapons warns against increasing nuclear risks and charts an alternative, non-nuclear course for the UK.*

My book *Security without Nuclear Deterrence*, a new edition of which Spokesman published last year in the UK, explains my gradual rejection of pro-nuclear deterrence indoctrination as a former operator of British nuclear weapons. In it I chronicle how the US politico-military industrial complex, drawing the wrong lessons from Hiroshima and Nagasaki and in denial about the horrors it had unleashed on humanity, seized upon the bogus mantra of nuclear deterrence to play upon people's fears and justify sustaining the unaccountable, highly profitable scientific and military monster spawned by the Manhattan Project.

Since then the principal guardians of nuclear deterrence – the western group comprising the US, UK and France – have struggled to provide intellectual coherence as endless adjustments to the theory and doctrine were made to accommodate the latest expansion of the nuclear arms race it had unleashed. Uncritical repetition by posturing political leaders, careerist experts and mainstream media of simplistic soundbites gave it the aura of a state religion, to the point where it echoed the fable of the emperor with no clothes.

Nuclear deterrence is based upon a crazy premise: that nuclear war can be made less probable by making it more probable. Worse, it is bedevilled by two insurmountable contradictions:

1. A rational leader cannot make a credible nuclear threat against an adversary capable of an invulnerable retaliatory 'second strike'.
2. Yet a second strike would be no more than posthumous revenge.

Moreover, unlike conventional war, following nuclear war – amid millions of dead and untreatable survivors, radioactive poisoning and apocalyptic destruction – the smoke alone from firestorms over cities in a nuclear war in South Asia would blot out the sun around the entire northern hemisphere, causing massive crop failure and global famine.

Recently, the groundless claim that nuclear weapons prevent war between nuclear-armed states was yet again challenged in the latest clashes between India and Pakistan, whereupon anxious nuclear powers led by the US and China had to intervene to restrain them. India and Pakistan naively followed their former colonial master's insistence that nuclear deterrence held the key to guaranteed security and acceptance as a great power. Instead, blind faith in nuclear deterrence has emboldened both sides to launch provocative military actions over disputed Kashmir: thus, nuclear weapons have increased the risk of war between them.

### Challenging the nuclear order

An article by British expert Dr Nick Ritchie, *A hegemonic nuclear order: Understanding the Ban Treaty and the power politics of nuclear weapons*, examines how the US-led nuclear order has evolved around nuclear deterrence.

The 2017 Treaty on the Prohibition of Nuclear Weapons (TPNW) represents a significant challenge to the P5's oligarchic power to establish norms biased towards non- and counter-proliferation, co-opt dissenters and institutions, and sustain mainstream acceptance of nuclear deterrence dogma.

This nuclear cartel recognises that reframing the discourse from an arms control and non-proliferation mindset to a 'humanitarian disarmament' standpoint threatens their status quo. Hence the ferocity of their response led by the western group, bitterly protesting at how irresponsibly naive the 122 member States who had adopted the TPNW had been in destabilising international security, when US-Russian relations were deteriorating, and North Korea had demonstrated further strides in its nuclear capability. This bluster tried to deflect attention from US President Trump's far more destabilising determination to renege on the Iran Joint Comprehensive Plan of Action, expand US ballistic missile defence, and even question the value to the US of NATO.

The Treaty on the Prohibition of Nuclear Weapons represents a new, determined diplomacy of resistance, fuelled by frustration over the nuclear cartel modernising their arsenals. The nuclear order is constrained by US ability to maintain subservience through bargaining between the dominant and dominated, employing strategies of inhibition applied to friends and foes alike, including aid, conventional arms sales, alliances and extended nuclear deterrence.

The post-Cold War period witnessed a shift from non- to counter-proliferation, preventing the acquisition of nuclear weapons by threatening attack against regional 'rogue' states, including first use with new low-yield nuclear warheads. In so doing, nuclear deterrence doctrine had been effectively inverted from professed prevention of war to pre-emptive war backed by ballistic missile defence, thereby exposing its practical irrelevance, not least in countering terrorism after 9/11.

Ritchie discusses how the western group have led development of benign conceptions of 'responsible' nuclear sovereignty and norms of behaviour, forming a respectable façade for what is essentially a fetishisation of nuclear weapons, imbuing them with extraordinary symbolic power. This subject was first tackled in 2009 by Anne Harrington de Santana in *Nuclear Weapons as the Currency of Power: Deconstructing the Fetishism of Force*. In support, institutions have been established to monitor and control nuclear weapon and energy programmes, such as the International Atomic Energy Agency, the 48-member Nuclear Suppliers Group, and the Zangger Committee with 39 member States. These institutions are not neutral, but politicised fora that fix systems of bias, privilege and inequality.

Other important US-dominated institutions include NATO and its Nuclear Planning Group, and the bilateral Asia-Pacific nuclear alliances. Then there is the institution of US-Russia nuclear arms limitation, developed to organise and constrain Cold War nuclear arms competition, manage the risk of nuclear violence in crises, and displace disarmament as the more logical, equitable and effective alternative path.

Closely linked to bilateral attempts at arms control is the US-Russia consensus to persist with over 1,500 strategic nuclear warheads on each side at minutes' notice to launch before confirmation of a nuclear strike, almost thirty years after the Cold War ended.

In a commendable effort to challenge this notoriously unreliable and irresponsible posture, a seminar held in Switzerland in 2009 co-sponsored by the East West Institute and the Swiss and New Zealand governments brought together US and Russian experts to explore ways to de-alert their forces. However, in their report, *Reframing Nuclear De-Alert: Decreasing the operational readiness of US and Russian nuclear arsenals*, the co-sponsors explained that no progress was achieved because both US and Russian sides blocked any change to current arrangements. This demonstrated the pernicious influence of nuclear deterrence doctrine and the associated nuclear order.

Underpinning this entire construct has been a deliberate socialisation of ideas to mould a pro-nuclear consensus, and sideline or suppress other ways of thinking about security, justice, and nuclear order through indoctrination, self-censorship, and exclusion of those 'out of touch with the real world' who do not accept nuclearism.

This regime of acceptable knowledge, or 'institutional truth', has brought us to the current perversely unsustainable situation, especially with the US erosion of arms control agreements. Western nuclear weapons are seen as inherently legitimate and good for international peace and security; but those in the hands of authoritarian states or those beyond the West's sphere of influence are illegitimate and undermine a western interpretation of international order.

### The nuclear deterrence and disarmament crisis

However, in addition to all nuclear-armed states modernising their arsenals, in February last year, the new US Nuclear Posture Review signalled the start of the most serious nuclear deterrence and disarmament crisis for 30 years.

In May 2018, Trump trashed the Iran Joint Comprehensive Plan of Action; then early this year the US released a Ballistic Missile Defence Review, and then withdrew from the Intermediate Nuclear Forces Treaty.

The 2018 US Nuclear Posture Review revives enthusiasm for 'usable' low-yield nuclear warheads to shore up nuclear deterrence credibility. It includes a new, low-yield Trident nuclear warhead; a new nuclear-armed cruise missile; and a more accurate, guided version of the B61 freefall nuclear bomb with lower variable yield between 0.3-50 kilotons (the Hiroshima bomb was 16 kilotons), and a fusing system more capable of withstanding the shock of penetrating hardened and deeply buried targets. This will replace 150 older model B61 bombs deployed in Belgium, Netherlands, Germany, Italy and Turkey.

The US Missile Defence Review, published in January 2019, commits the US to expanding ground and space-based systems. These violate the fundamental principles of Mutual Assured Destruction – but there seems to be a lack of awareness, let alone alarm, about this in mainstream western commentaries.

One new, particularly dangerous development is the push to deploy conventionally armed ballistic missiles in US submarines, possibly including Trident, for pre-emptive 'Prompt Global Strike' against a threat which otherwise would require a nuclear response. An obvious risk would be that, even if the conventional warhead is launched in a different ballistic missile from Trident, Russia would presume it was a nuclear strike.

## A global nuclear tinderbox

The announcement on 2 February of US withdrawal from the 1987 Intermediate-range Nuclear Forces Treaty, followed the next day by Russia's withdrawal, means that the world – especially Europe – is faced with a far more dangerous rerun of the 1979 NATO decision to deploy nuclear-armed Cruise missiles and Pershing ballistic missiles in Europe to counter Soviet SS-20 intermediate range ballistic missiles.

This time the US leadership is unlikely to listen to European concerns, which are heightened by a more ambiguous US/NATO nuclear posture; probable collapse of US-Russian arms control initiatives, and even greater consequent public alarm and resistance. This could severely strain NATO cohesion, and trigger a major rethink of its nuclear deterrence doctrine.

In predictable response, specifically to Trump's withdrawal from the INF Treaty, President Vladimir Putin claimed in his state of the nation address on 20 February 2019 that, in addition to new weapon systems soon to become operational, Russian submarines stationed off the east and west US coasts are now capable of launching Zircon hypersonic stealthy cruise missiles invulnerable to ballistic missile defence with a range of up to 1,000 km.

The inevitable consequence of US hubristic abuse of its hegemonic nuclear order, and the Russian response, is to increase the risk of nuclear weapon use through miscalculation, mistake or malfunction.

Moreover, there is general acceptance that once the first nuclear detonation occurs, escalation to all-out nuclear war would rapidly and uncontrollably follow. Facilitating all this has been a fallacious and disingenuous lumping together of nuclear with chemical and biological weapons of mass destruction by some policy-makers, when the reality is that nuclear weapons are orders of magnitude worse.

Britain is the best-placed nuclear weapon state to lead the world out of the new nuclear deterrence and disarmament crisis. The UK nuclear arsenal is the smallest of the P5, deployed in only one system, at several days' notice to fire; a £70 billion Defence Budget deficit, driven by planned Trident renewal related to dependence on the US, would grow with Brexit; and the £50 billion opportunity cost of Trident renewal could be redirected to providing a more balanced, useful Royal Navy contribution to graduated conventional deterrence.

Meanwhile, Opposition Leader Jeremy Corbyn has experienced no loss of public support on pledging that, if he became Prime Minister, he would refuse to authorise nuclear weapon use, and would sign the Treaty on the Prohibition of Nuclear Weapons. In addition, there is a solid anti-nuclear majority in Scotland, where British nuclear weapons are based, linked to support for independence. Finally, a network of legal, academic and political experts and former RN operators of nuclear weapons are working in support of a determined, experienced group of campaigners opposing the UK Government's unlawful and irresponsible nuclear posture.

If the UK were to reject nuclear deterrence, the British and international anti-nuclear movements, and an overwhelming majority of world opinion, would erupt in support. As initiator, organiser and energiser of a process that would start to shift western attitudes from the current adversarial national security paradigm to one embracing co-operative security, the UK would gain a global role in which it would be welcomed as truly a 'force for good'.

The first anti-nuclear breakout by one of the P5 would be sensational and would transform the nuclear disarmament debate overnight. In NATO, Britain would wield unprecedented influence in leading the drive for a non-nuclear strategy – which must happen if NATO is to sustain its cohesion. It would create new openings for shifting the mindset in the US and France, and give pause to India and Pakistan, as well as others seeking nuclear weapons. Moreover, it would open the way for a major reassessment by Russia and China of their nuclear strategies, for all nuclear forces to be de-alerted, and for multilateral negotiations to start on a Nuclear Weapons Convention.

### Britain should lead France away from nuclear deterrence

Some political and military diehards argue that it is critical for Britain to retain nuclear weapons because 'France must never be allowed to be the sole European nuclear power'. My response is that the security threats confronting British and fellow Europeans in the twenty-first century demand that both the UK and France move on at last from the Napoleonic Wars and loss of Empires.

As the first medium-sized power to acquire nuclear weapons, Britain has the opportunity to set France a wiser and more responsible example. Central to this are the opportunity costs for both countries' defence policies. Above all, the ridiculous notion that France's greatness depends on possession of nuclear weapons should be exposed as demeaning to French citizens and culture. The reality is that threatening nuclear weapon use risks the annihilation of both French and British culture within devastated and poisoned homelands.

### A new British challenge to 'pressing the nuclear button'

Since the 1990s, when UK nuclear weapons were de-targeted and placed at relaxed notice to fire, a decision to re-target, let alone use, UK Trident would initiate the most extreme use of British military force, with unprecedented political and legal implications.

A 2016 report by Sir John Chilcot on lessons to be learned from the disastrous 2003 US-UK invasion of Iraq recommended that Parliament should be more involved in a decision to go to war. A Parliamentary Inquiry by the Public Administration and Constitutional Affairs Select Committee is currently probing how best to implement this. A former distinguished British Polaris submarine Commander, Robert Forsyth, has made recommending establishment of an advisory committee, independent of Government, to scrutinise the political and legal justifications for a re-targeting or firing order from the Prime Minister [see *Spokesman 141]*.

Commander Forsyth's concern is that the currently deployed UK Trident-armed submarine Commanding Officer, who is acutely aware that what he is there to do is to actually 'press the nuclear button' on behalf of the Prime Minister, would be placed in legal jeopardy by current British nuclear policy. Nuremberg Principle IV states:

'The fact that a person acted pursuant to order of his government or superior does not relieve him from responsibility under international law, provided a moral choice was in fact possible for him.'

Interestingly, Admiral Lord Alan West, testifying to the Inquiry as First Sea Lord during the invasion of Iraq, endorsed Cdr Forsyth's concern. And of course, the reality is that there is no scenario where a 100 kiloton UK Trident warhead could ever be used lawfully.

A most timely article, *The Finger on the Button — The Authority to Use Nuclear Weapons in Nuclear-Armed States*, was published in February by the James Martin Center for Nonproliferation Studies, Monterey. Prompted by concerns over US President Trump's nuclear threats to North Korea's President Kim Jong-un, the authors Jeffrey Lewis and Bruno Tertrais compare who is authorised to initiate nuclear weapon use and the related procedures in each of the nine known nuclear-armed States.

However, re-targeting is not mentioned, and there is little discussion of accountability, especially the need to justify use and scrutinise legality. Yet at least one US Trident submarine Commanding Officer has indicated that, in the event of a peacetime order to launch, he would insist on confirmation and a justification. Also, there is no mention of recent public statements by current and ex-Chiefs of US Strategic Command challenging an illegal firing order.

Meanwhile, when I last met Bruno Tertrais, a veteran commentator and former adviser to the French Ministry of Defence, I asked him what impact British breakout from nuclear deterrence would have in France. He replied: 'It would make the French think objectively about nuclear weapons for the first time'.

To conclude, in my view the most ground breaking achievement of the Treaty on the Prohibition of Nuclear Weapons is to have provoked the US-led nuclear cartel to drop any attempt to conceal its irresponsible, dishonest manipulation of nuclear deterrence theory and doctrine, with associated dangers to global security. This is why, in my recent TEDx talk on the insanity of nuclear deterrence, I risked telling it like it is:

> 'Nuclear deterrence is no more than a repulsive, unlawful protection racket used as a counterfeit currency of power. It is hugely profitable to the corporate arms industry. The power elites of the nuclear-armed states are in denial that their game of nuclear chicken really does risk the survival of us all. But the tide of history is at last turning towards justice. It is time for all of us to step up and end the threat to humanity and the planet from this irresponsible hoax holding us all hostage.'

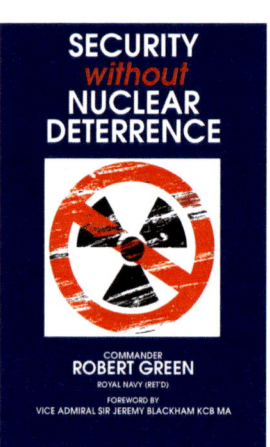

# Spokesman Books: Popular Titles

### The Washington Connection and Third World Fascism
*The Political Economy of Human Rights, Volume 1*
**Noam Chomsky and Edward S. Herman**

This landmark text argues with devastating logic and overwhelming documentation that the purpose of US global policy is to make the world safe for exploitation by US corporate interests and that this has required and continues to require the installation and support of brutal military/police dictatorships throughout the Third World. It also requires an apologetic ideology which portrays all this as being in the highest interests of democracy and human rights.

Price: £17.95 | 414 pages | Paperback | ISBN: 978 0 85124 2484

### Delinquent Genius
*The Strange Affair of Man and His Technology*
**Mike Cooley**

"Delinquent Genius is simply brimming with insights. It traces the sources of technology and its application. It is, above all else, a brilliant account of a dangerous hubris which can lead to that which is instrumental becoming a source, a dangerous source of domination, of passive rather than active existence..."
Michael D. Higgins, President of Ireland

Price: £11.99 | 248 pages | Paperback | ISBN: 978 0 85124 8783

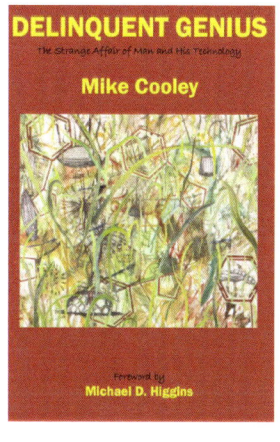

### Kettling the Unions?
*A Guide to the 2016 Trade Union Act*
**Alan Tuckman**

"This very welcome book is intended to provide an analysis of the roots of the Trade Union Act 2016. Those roots lie in Thatcher's legislation of the 1980s and further back to the undermining of collective bargaining in UK industrial relations that developed in the 1970s, in the context of neoliberalism's rise to dominance. ."
Mark Serwotka, General Secretary, PCS Union

Price: £14.99 | 204 pages | Paperback | ISBN: 978 0 85124 8745

# www.spokesmanbooks.com

# Continuously at sea

*Ronnie Cowan MP*
*Carol Monaghan MP*
*Caroline Lucas MP*
*Deidre Brock MP*

*In April 2019, Members of the Westminster Parliament debated 'continuous at-sea deterrence' (CASD), which for 50 years has seen nuclear-armed Royal Navy submarines slowly patrol the oceans. Several speeches stand out, particularly those by Members who live with nuclear weapons on their doorsteps. We reprint some extracts.*

◄ Westminster Abbey, 3 May 2019, dieing quietly at CASD anniversary service

**Ronnie Cowan (Inverclyde, Scottish National Party):** … When I rose to make my maiden speech on 1 July 2015, I touched on the Trident programme, because it is close to my heart. In fact, it is very close to my constituency. At the time, I mentioned that Trident seemed to be a bit of an abstract concept. People know it is out there, but they do not know what it is, how much it costs, how much it cannot be used, and what it is actually doing as a deterrent.

If you stand on the shore of my constituency, you will often see Vanguard class submarines moving silently through the deep waters. They catch the sunlight, which shimmers along their long, sleek, black bodies as they cut through the surface of the water. Their colour may suggest giant eels, but they lack the elegance. They are, however, engineering marvels. It takes some doing to fire a missile from beneath the water's surface, project it through the water until it breaks free, and manage two controlled explosions that project the missile to a pre-defined target where ballistic missiles carrying nuclear warheads are released and either explode on impact or are exploded automatically at the required height to cause maximum death and destruction. Mankind has never lacked ingenuity when it comes to inventing ways of killing each other. I cannot help but wonder what else we could have achieved with all that time, effort, ingenuity and money.

The issue we have is that successive Governments of the United Kingdom have supported and expanded the nuclear weapons programme at eye-watering cost. Why? When I sit in the House of Commons, I talk to many Members who support Trident. I can tell them that these weapons can kill tens of millions of people. But they know that. I can tell them that the watershed will be poisoned, crops will fail and many more will die in the most degrading ways from famine, pestilence and plague. But they know that. I can share stories of survivors, such as Setsuko Thurlow, who told me of people falling to the ground, bellies extended and bursting as they hit the ground, of people trying to carry their own eyes that had fallen out of their heads, and of people with their flesh falling off their bones as they died in agony.

I can also tell Members that weapons of mass destruction have not stopped wars across the globe from Vietnam to Afghanistan. But they know that. I can tell them that WMD are no protection from terrorism. But they know that. I can tell them that the £205 billion could be spent on health, education, housing, transport or even financing our conventional armed forces. But they know that too.

The majority of supporters of weapons of mass destruction are just like me with one vital difference. They believe that WMD are a deterrent. They believe their existence has kept us safe. As those weapons have existed during a period in which we have avoided wars on the scale of the First and Second World Wars, I can see where they are coming from. If people believe that keeping their guard up is keeping them safe, then lowering their guard is a frightening thing to do. In this case, they are so frightened that they are prepared to carry out the greatest atrocity humankind has ever perpetrated, and have it done in their name. Well, not in my name. Not all countries believe that nuclear warfare is required. Maybe as many as nine countries feel the need to have nuclear weapons, out of 200.

**Carol Monaghan (Glasgow North West, Scottish National Party):**
I start by declaring an interest. My husband served on Trident submarines for most of his 17-year service in the Royal Navy. His final post before retiring was as the weapon engineer officer on *HMS Victorious*. He brought her through refit in Devonport and sea trials from Faslane, and he carried out the firing during the 2009 demonstration and shakedown operation [DASO] off the coast of Florida ...

Following the DASO firing, *Victorious* re-entered full service and, following an extremely busy year, the crew carried out a deterrence patrol over Christmas 2009. It gives me great pleasure to say that my granny's Christmas tree went on that patrol. When my husband finally left *Victorious*, he forgot to take my granny's Christmas tree. I wonder if any crew members would be able to confirm whether that Christmas tree – a little white optical fibre fellow – is still on board. For the role he played, my husband received the Commander-in-Chief, Fleet commendation, an award that still hangs proudly in our home in Whiteinch in Glasgow.

Despite my pride in my husband's service, my opposition to Trident has been constant. As a teenager my views were formed over the Cold War and fears of mutually assured destruction, and my earliest political campaigns, long before I ever thought to consider Scottish independence, were against Trident. Over time the indiscriminate nature of these weapons, which are designed to cause such widespread devastation, has meant that I will never support Trident or its successor. That is regardless of whether we can afford these platforms, which, to be frank, as conventional forces are being cut to the bone, we cannot. In fact, our maritime capabilities are so depleted that we no longer have any major warships based in Scotland. This is at a time when threats from Russia are at their greatest for a generation. We have repeatedly had to rely on our allies when incursions occur. On at least two occasions in 2016, Russian submarines were suspected of operating off Faslane, and the UK had to seek assistance from its allies to help track those intruders. Those incursions fit a pattern of Russia testing defences and seeking crucial information about the Vanguard boats, namely the acoustic signature that allows them to be tracked. If Russia were able to obtain a recording of the signature, it would have serious implications for the UK's deterrent.

Are we increasing conventional capabilities to help deal with that? No: we decided to scrap the entire fleet of Nimrods. Although the Nimrods will eventually be replaced by the P-8, the first of which is expected in Lossiemouth in 2020, we have been playing Russian roulette for the past 10 years and will continue to do so unless we increase conventional capabilities, particularly around the north of Scotland. If we were to find ourselves under attack, as has happened in Crimea, our defences are being whittled down to two options: we can either nuke them or chase them away with pitchforks. How on earth does that make us safer?

The hon. Member for Stirling (Stephen Kerr) said that the SNP does not speak for Scotland. Okay, we may not speak for some of Scotland, but our position on Trident is supported by the Scottish Government, the Scottish Labour Party, the Scottish Greens, the Church of Scotland, the Catholic Church in Scotland and Scottish civil society. I would suggest that it is the Tories who are out of kilter with the Scottish people.

This is a debate to commemorate the 50th anniversary of the continuous at-sea deterrent. I take no pleasure in the money and resources that have been funnelled into this vanity project, which allows Britain to have a seat at the big boys' table at the UN, to the detriment of other parts of our armed forces. I take no pleasure in the money that is thrown into the maintenance and into the successor project, while at the same time child poverty is at the highest level that many of us have seen in our lifetime.

I pay tribute to the men, and now women, who have made the commitment to serve. People often talk about the difficulties of separation and the three-month patrols, but those who have a partner on one of the boats will know that in many ways the patrol is the most settled time. The work-up period and testing, false starts and defects mean that families cope with massive upheaval in the lead up to the actual patrol, repeatedly saying big bye-byes only to have partners return the next day and children not really knowing whether this is the time that daddy will disappear. That puts enormous strain on families and relationships—a strain that is not always recognised.

It is time that the MoD considered the realities of modern-day families. In the past, partners and families would live close to the base with a ready-made support network. Recognising that spouses have their own careers is important to a modern-day armed forces.

Submariners do an incredible job and are the most highly skilled personnel in the armed forces. They have many career options on leaving, so retention issues leave serious skill shortages in the submarine service. The MOD has said that no submarine goes to sea without the minimum complement of suitably qualified and experienced personnel required to operate the boat safely, and that vacancies are managed to ensure that safety and operational capability is never compromised, but that is done off the back of submariners. Severe shortages of suitably skilled personnel meant that, in my husband's last year in the Navy, he had six days' leave. That included weekends. That is simply not sustainable. There comes a point when pride in serving cannot make up for poor conditions of service. Ultimately, many choose between service and seeing their children grow up. I argue that despite the money being thrown at Trident, its ultimate demise will be caused by a failure to support the personnel and by gaps in critical skills.

As we mark 50 years of the continuous at-sea deterrent and recognise the dedication of those serving in the silent service, I say that the time has come to invest properly in cyber, in conventional defence and in our personnel. Despite campaigning actively against the platform, I and my hon. Friends pay tribute to those who have served, and to those who continue to serve.

**Caroline Lucas (Brighton Pavilion, Green Party):** It is a real pleasure and honour to follow the hon. Member for Glasgow North West (Carol Monaghan), because she speaks with real authority and eloquence about these issues. I am happy to speak as well in my capacity as chair of the cross-party group on nuclear disarmament. Let me put it on the record at the top of my speech that I am very happy to pay tribute to the submariners for their service to this country and to their families for the sacrifice that they make, which the hon. Lady has set out very clearly.

I do not think that there is any contradiction between paying tribute to that service and also being very clear that, for me, nuclear weapons are abhorrent. Others have said during this debate that it is inconsistent to have a nuclear deterrent if we are not prepared to use it. I absolutely agree with that, and I am very proud to say that I would not, under any circumstances, use nuclear weapons, and still less would I support the Prime Minister's position of a first use of nuclear weapons. I believe that nuclear weapons are indiscriminate, illegal and obscene.

Let us just think what that first strike, which the Prime Minister was so proud not to rule out, could really mean. The heart of a nuclear explosion reaches a temperature of several million degrees centigrade. Over a wide area, the resulting heat flash literally vaporises all human tissue. At Hiroshima, within a radius of half a mile, the only remains of the people caught in the open were their shadows burned into stone. People inside buildings will be indirectly killed by the blast and the heat effects as buildings collapse and all inflammable materials burst into flames. The immediate death rate in that area will be over 90%. Individual fires will combine to produce a fire storm as all the oxygen is consumed. As the heat rises, air is drawn in from the periphery at or near ground level. This results in lethal hurricane-force winds and perpetuates the fire as the fresh oxygen is burned. The contamination will continue potentially for hundreds of thousands of years. The Red Cross has estimated that 1 billion people around the world could face starvation as a result of a nuclear war.

Let me be very clear: I hate all war, but there is something particular about nuclear war. Simply saying that it is in the same category as other forms of war is wrong. What is wrong as well is to say that we cannot uninvent things that have already been invented. We saw what happened when it came to chemical weapons, biological weapons and cluster munitions being banned. If there was more support from countries such as the UK, nuclear weapons could be banned as well. There was the UN treaty on the prohibition of nuclear weapons, and I found it frankly outrageous that the UK Government could not even be bothered to turn up to the talks. That was a campaign that was run throughout the world. One hundred and twenty two countries supported the nuclear ban treaty. The International Campaign to Abolish Nuclear Weapons won the Nobel peace prize for its efforts. The treaty is a strong and comprehensive text, with the potential to achieve a world without nuclear weapons. It opened for signature in September 2017 and will enter into force when 50 states have ratified it. It has so far been signed by 70 states and ratified by 22, and more and more are signing up.

I want to counter the argument made from the Labour Benches that the treaty is somehow not multilateral. It is, not least because there is no requirement for a country to join; there is no requirement on a country to have forgone their nuclear weapons before joining. If the UK had used its considerable clout on the world stage to have really shown some leadership on this issue, there could have been at least a chance of getting the countries around the table to have gone away and begun the process multilaterally of getting rid of their weapons.

… It is very easy to characterise those of us who are against nuclear weapons as somehow not living in the real world, so perhaps I could just remind the House that there are plenty of people within the military world who do not think that nuclear weapons are a useful tool going forward. Back in 2014 senior political and diplomatic figures—including people such as the former Conservative Foreign Secretary Sir Malcolm Rifkind, former Defence Secretary Des Browne and former Foreign Secretary Lord Owen—came together with very high ranking military personnel to say that they believe that the risks posed by nuclear weapons and the international dynamics that could lead to nuclear weapons being used are being underestimated, and that those risks are insufficiently understood by world leaders.

The Government's main argument for replacing Trident appears to be that it is the ultimate insurance in an uncertain world. I argue that they fail to acknowledge that it is our very possession of nuclear weapons that is making that world more uncertain. Nor have the advocates of nuclear weapons ever explained why, if Trident is so vital to protecting us, that is not also the case for every other country in the world. The Secretary of State did not answer me at the beginning of this debate—it seems a long time ago now—when I put it to him that we have no moral arguments to put to other countries to ask them not to acquire nuclear weapons if we ourselves are not only keeping them but upgrading them. I put it to him again that a world in which every country is striving for, and potentially achieving, nuclear weapons would be an awful lot more dangerous than the world we have today.

… So far there has been very little recognition in this debate of the fact that nuclear weapons systems are themselves fallible. According to a shocking report by Chatham House, there have been 13 incidents since

1962 in which nuclear weapons have very nearly been launched. One of the most dramatic, in 1983, was when Stanislav Petrov, the duty officer in a Soviet nuclear war early-warning centre, found his system warning of the launch of five US missiles. After a few moments of agonising, he judged it, thankfully and correctly, to be a false alarm. If he had reached a different conclusion and passed the information up the control chain, that could have triggered the firing of nuclear missiles from Russia.

**Deidre Brock (Edinburgh North and Leith, Scottish National Party):** Parliamentary questions I have asked uncovered the shocking fact that since 2006 there have been 789 nuclear safety incidents at Coulport and Faslane, and half of the incidents at Faslane have taken place in just the past four years. Does the hon. Lady agree that it is a very serious worry that nuclear safety incidents are on the rise under the watch of a Government who should not have control of a TV remote, let alone the most dangerous weapons on the planet?

**Caroline Lucas:** I thank the hon. Lady for her intervention. She rightly shines a spotlight on issues that far too rarely get covered in the media or even in debates such as this one.

The UK Government have shamefully refused to participate in the treaty negotiations I have been describing while nevertheless claiming that they share the goal of a nuclear weapons-free world. But it is not too late to make amends. The Government should now engage constructively and work towards signing that treaty and supporting the global moves towards the total elimination of nuclear weapons. That, unlike a willingness to launch nuclear weapons and incinerate millions of innocent people, or to waste billions on a weapon that will never be used and therefore serves no evident purpose, would be the true test of a Prime Minister's leadership.

*Bertrand and Edith Russell at Bow Street Magistrates Court, September 1961.*
*They were sent to prison for taking part in sit-down protests against nuclear weapons.*

# Win we must

*Bertrand Russell*

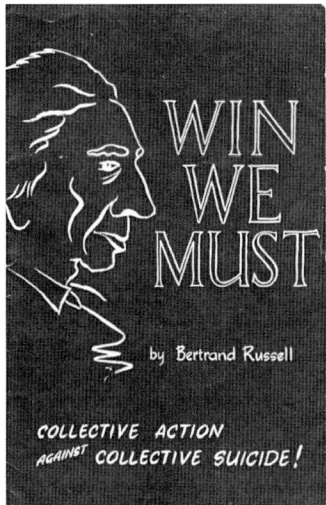

*Adding some perspective to current concerns, Russell's anti-nuclear broadside was delivered in Birmingham in March 1961 and subsequently published as a pamphlet by the organisers of the Second Midlands Conference for Peace.*

My purpose in the remarks which I shall be making is to place the British agitation against nuclear armaments within the framework of the situation in the world. Our movement is part – but only part – of a world-wide movement to persuade mankind to abstain from collective suicide. Collective suicide, given the present known weapons of mass destruction, can only be prevented by collective action. Nothing that any one country can do in isolation will bring safety to any part of the world. If our movement against British reliance on nuclear weapons is to be effective in diminishing the peril which now threatens all nations, this result can only be achieved through international repercussions of what our own country does. Our main purpose must be to prevent a war using weapons of mass destruction – and not only to prevent it for a time by makeshift devices, but to establish such institutions in the world as shall make it reasonably certain that a war of extermination will not occur in the foreseeable future.

### What would happen?

It is, to my mind, amazing and profoundly saddening that there should be any human beings who advocate a state of affairs that makes nuclear war not unlikely. What, exactly, would happen if a general nuclear war broke out is, fortunately, as yet unknown. It may be that such a war would put an end to human life entirely. It may be that there would be survivors in the most southerly of inhabited regions. It may be that there would be some survivors in Europe and Asia and North America. American governmental experts who take the most optimistic view that is al all plausible have published horrifying figures. In 1958, the US Secretary of Defence, summarising a Pentagon report, maintained that, in such a war, 160 million people would be killed in the United States, 200 million in the USSR, and everybody in Britain and Western Europe. Nothing has occurred since to modify this estimate, which is the most governmentally authoritative estimate available.

## Madness

How is such a war to be prevented? Each side has a simple answer: it is only necessary, we are told, that our side should be stronger than the other, since we are friends of peace and would not initiate a war even if we were sure of victory. The trouble for this formula is that it is impossible for each side to be stronger than the other. So long as each side believes that this is the way to secure peace, the only result is an armament race which must first reduce the populations of East and West to subsistence level and, in the end, is almost certain to produce actual war. Many people tell us that, however much each side goes on piling up armaments, there will never actually be a war because that would be madness. I agree emphatically that it would be madness, but I do not agree that is a reason for expecting it not to occur. Many careful studies have been made in America, and almost all of them have concluded that, if the present policies persist, a nuclear war is more likely than not. This, for instance, is the conclusion of Oskar Morgenstern, a politically orthodox American defence expert. It is also the conclusion reached by a committee of experts appointed by Ohio State University to examine precisely this issue. Quite recently, Lord Hailsham, our Minister of Science, unequivocally pronounced the same sense. What is strange and perplexing is that, nevertheless, many of these experts do not draw the conclusion that present policies ought to be changed. I think it is probably true that neither America nor Russia would deliberately inaugurate a general nuclear war, but there are various ways, some of them terrifyingly probable, by which a general war could come about without the deliberate intention of any government.

## War by accident

One of the most probable of these is war by accident or by misunderstanding. Our Prime Minister, in terms of dogmatic certainty, has pronounced: '*There will be no war by accident.*' It seems charitable to suppose that he believed this when he said it; but if he did, he was ignorant of things which it was his duty to know. The danger of unintended war arises, at present, mainly through the American doctrine of instant retaliation. American military authorities believe – or pretend to believe –

that, at any moment, Russia may make a surprise attack upon NATO countries. There is not a shred of evidence for such a view, and very strong evidence against it, but it is held and proclaimed and made the basis of American strategy. Radar stations in Canada, Greenland, Yorkshire, and many other places, are perpetually on the look out for approaching Russian missiles. They have frequently misinterpreted flights of birds as approaching bombs and, on at least one occasion, they mistook the moon for a Russian attack. Whenever a mistake of this sort occurs, American airmen armed with bombs get into the air. They have practised such speed that they can now be off the ground within two minutes of receiving the warning signal. Hitherto, mistakes have been discovered in time, but this is a piece of luck, upon which it would be most imprudent to rely. If one key man is drunk or insane or suddenly ill, the mistake may not be discovered. Since the Russians, like the Americans, expect a surprise attack and also believe in instant retaliation, one such mistake may easily precipitate a full scale war.

## Polaris

Polaris submarines which are being stationed in Holy Loch increase the danger of accidental war. It is claimed that they can voyage anywhere without being detected by the Russians. Their bombs are always in instant readiness. Their captains receive orders direct from Washington. In the event of war, these orders might not get through, and each captain would have to act on his own initiative. It might easily happen that through some mechanical defect the captain failed to receive expected messages and concluded that war had broken out. In that case, it would break out.

These are only samples of the danger, which also takes various other forms. The danger is so great that every day during which we still exist is a subject of thankfulness; and, although disaster on any one day is not probable, disaster in the long run is almost certain unless new, radical measures are adopted.

What the world needs is obvious to every sane and informed man. It needs the abolition of all weapons of mass destructions – nuclear, chemical and biological. It needs an immense lessening of East-West tension and of the mutual suspicion that is engendered by tension. It needs a world-wide authority with power to arbitrate on vexed questions in any part of the world. Above all, it needs a general realisation that war has become an insanity which cannot secure anything that any belligerent can desire, for, if this is not generally realised, suspicion will remain and each bloc will fear that the other is evading whatever disarmament treaties may have been concluded.

All this is what the world needs if the human race is to survive. What can Britain do to further these international aims?

## Unilateralism

The policy that we advocate is called 'unilateralism', but, unless accompanied by some explanations, this name for our policy is somewhat misleading. We want multilateral disarmament, but we think that British unilateral disarmament is the most effective step that Britain can take towards that end. This conclusion has been forced upon us by the utter failure of all disarmament conferences since the end of the last war. We have been reluctantly forced to the conclusion that the West, at least, has not been sincere about disarmament and has made only such offers as it was confident the East would reject. Once, in 1955, the insincerity of the West was dramatically exposed: the West made some excellent proposals towards disarmament, but, to the horror of the Western Powers, the Soviet Government accepted these proposals, whereupon the West at once withdrew them.

## The Soviet attitude

At the present time, Russia is urging complete and speedy nuclear disarmament. Apart from the repeated statements by Khrushchev, the Russian position has been set forth unequivocally in an article by Major General Talenski called 'The Character of Modern War' (printed in English in *Survival* for January-February, 1961) which announced: 'War in the military-technical sense has outlived itself as a weapons of policy.' 'We must,' he concludes, 'struggle even more stubbornly and consistently for the destruction of all armaments, for the exclusion of war from the life of human society, for peace in the whole world.' This attitude of the Soviet Government has made Western governmental circles very angry, since they cannot see how to resist it without giving Russia a great propaganda advantage. American military authorities evaded the issue when it was new by means of the U-2 incident, and it is to be feared that something similar may dash the hopes of sane men whenever there is a danger of agreement. It is this constant failure of attempts at multilateral disarmament which has persuaded many of the friends of peace in Britain to advocate British unilateral disarmament without waiting for general agreement. In addition to this incentive, British unilateralists have, however, a number of other reasons in favour of their policy. I will enumerate four of them.

## A neutral Britain

(1) The plan, which has hitherto been pursued, of having conferences between NATO and the Warsaw Pact alone has the great disadvantage that each side comes with a prepared plan and, for reasons of prestige, feels that it must not yield an inch to the plan of the other side. It is obvious that this is an ideal method of not reaching agreement, and entirely convenient to the military authorities and the armaments industry. But, if disarmament is really desired, it is not a sensible method. It would be far better to invite neutrals to draw up a scheme which should be strictly impartial between East and West, and which, since it would spring from neutrals, each side could accept without loss of face. For this reason, there is more hope of solving the world's problems by the initiative of neutrals than by acrimonious disputations between East and West alone. If Britain became neutral, Britain could take part in this work of conciliation by organising, and perhaps leading, a group of politically mature uncommitted Powers. Those who wish Britain to adopt neutrality and unilateral nuclear disarmament are often accused of urging Britain to abdicate responsibility. This is the exact opposite of the truth. Britain's responsibility to the world cannot be adequately fulfilled while Britain is tied to NATO and is supposed, however fallaciously, to be protected by American nuclear power. Britain as the leader of a group of neutrals, inspired by the hope of peace, can do a work of immeasurable value in resolving the present deadlock and urging upon both sides such measures of conciliation as will remove the pall of terror which now darkens the world.

(2) Even if it were true – which it is not – that nuclear weapons protect us, it would still be abominable to depend upon such protection. When American military authorities tell us that in a nuclear war there will be 160 million American deaths and 200 million Russian deaths, we are expected to deplore the 160 million but rejoice at the 200 million, so that, on balance, we are to feel pleasure at the holocaust. It is considered wicked and a sign of Communist tendencies to remember that Russians are human beings and that a nuclear death is as painful to them as to us. I find it unbearable, as I go about my daily business, to think that I owe my continued existence to my Government's capacity of unimaginably vast slaughter. It is not by means of such ferocity that a good world can be built.

## Protection illusory

(3) But the protection afforded by H-bombs is not only wicked. It is also illusory. This is especially true as regards Britain and other allies of the US. At the time of the U-2 incident, Khrushchev and Malinovsky informed

the world, in characteristically vigorous language, that allies of the United States which allowed their territory to be used by America for what Russia considered unfriendly acts ran a risk of obliteration. Orthodox American military authorities pointed out that Britain, or any other ally of America, could be completely exterminated by Russia in about half-an-hour, and that, in spite of NATO, it is very unlikely that America would avenge our extinction by proceeding to extinguish the rest of mankind. At most, two per cent of Russian bombs would be needed to put an end to Britain. And, while Britain allows America to make use of her territory for purposes hostile to Russia, Russia might conceivably feel impelled to such action. This would not be the case if Britain were neutral. It follows that our reliance upon American protection, so far from making us safer, in fact makes us less safe. Our membership of NATO is, therefore, not only wicked, but also foolish. I do not pretend that, as neutrals, we should be safe. But I do say with all imaginable emphasis that we should be less unsafe than we are at present.

### Britain and NATO

(4) There are those who argue that our membership of NATO increases the strength of the alliance and, therefore, diminishes the likelihood of a war initiated by Russia. This is, in every respect, a fallacious argument. We do not add anything appreciable to the strength of America by our alliance. On the contrary, we saddle America with a very onerous obligation to protect us. Every humane person must hope that America would not fulfil this obligation, since the attempt to do so would only make death world-wide instead of merely British. This view is taken by military authorities in America, but is rejected by British military authorities, not upon any rational grounds, but only because it is humiliating to British pride. There is a further fallacy in the argument: ever since the death of Stalin, Russia has been less inclined to war than America and, if it were indeed the case that we added appreciably to the strength of NATO, we should be increasing the likelihood of general war by belonging to the more bellicose side.

Some authorities, especially in America, endeavour to persuade their readers that something tolerable may survive a nuclear war. The most detailed of these is Mr. Herman Kahn who believes, or pretends to believe, that the economies of both America and Russia might recover, perhaps within ten years. One gathers – though on this point he is not explicit – that, as soon as they have sufficiently recovered, they are to prepare to fight again. And, after a second nuclear war, if Mr. Kahn is right, there may be a third and perhaps a fourth, and so on, until there are not enough people alive to build H-bombs. If on the other hand, Mr. Kahn supposes that, after a nuclear war, which has given no supremacy to either, both sides will be ready to negotiate a secure peace, there can be no reason why they should not negotiate a peace without first having a war.

There can be no certainty as to the magnitude of the destruction which a full-scale war would bring about. Some think that the whole human race would perish. Others maintain that, while all the great nations of the northern hemisphere would lose social cohesion and be reduced to small marauding bands, the southern hemisphere would fare better and a new culture might be developed, presumably under the leadership of the South African White. This view is taken by Fred Charles Iklé in his book *The Social Impact of Bomb Destruction*:

'Those speculatively inclined, then, ought to picture the world, after an all-out nuclear war with extreme fallout contamination, not as a planet inhabited only by lower forms of plant life immune to radioactivity, but as a world with expanding populations and perhaps thriving economies in South America, South Africa, Indonesia, Australia, and New Zealand. From this picture one might try to look still farther ahead and perhaps reach the conclusion that the surviving generations would be farther away from a peaceful millennium than ever, because of the deep racial, religious, and ideological differences that divide the peoples of the Southern hemisphere. Indeed – this speculation could continue – both capitalism and communism might survive, since both might be represented among the survivor nations. But the powerful states which fought for these issues would have disappeared from history – much as the Inca Empire and the realm of Carthage have ended forever.'

As for North America, the most cheerful prophecy which seems to have any kind of justification is that of John M. Fowler in a book called *Fallout* which has a preface by Adlai Stevenson. Mr. Fowler says:

'A skilled and resourceful individual or family outside the ring of complete destruction and on the outskirts of the lethal umbrella of fallout might survive the nightmarish early weeks. By burrowing into the walls of the basement or huddling under some hastily improvised shield in a corner, a person might survive although the outdoors was an oven of silent death.'

Such statements represent the extreme of hope that is in any degree reasonable. Nevertheless, when there were Congressional hearings about the possible effects of nuclear war, the newspaper reports, we are told, were pervaded by a 'spirit of optimism' [sic] on the basis that some human beings might survive. I find it impossible to understand the mentality of those who regard such a prospect as cheerful, especially as the war they envisage would do nothing towards establishing the sort of world that they profess to desire.

## A silly suggestion

One is almost driven to the conclusion that many people hate the prospect of a world without war and will invent any argument, however flimsy, to persuade men that war need not be abolished. One of the silliest suggestions in this direction is that Russia and America might agree not to employ H-bombs, but to conduct their future wars as if nuclear weapons had never been invented. It is remarkable that those who make this suggestion are among those who proclaim most loudly the complete untrustworthiness of the Soviet Government. It must be obvious to anybody who has seen war-passions in operation that, if either side was in danger of defeat, it would employ H-bombs if it had them whatever agreements to the contrary might exist.

## A cruel hoax

Another plan for persuading populations that the destructiveness of nuclear warfare can be kept within bounds is what is called 'civil defence.' I find it impossible to speak with any moderation about this cruel and murderous hoax. Mr. Kahn, with the approval of many military authorities, suggests that the United States should spend 30 billion dollars on civil defence. As we know, America is in one respect more fortunate than Britain since, when the radar chain is completed, Americans will have 25 minutes' warning that the bombs are on the way, whereas Britain will have only four minutes. The purpose of these schemes is to persuade the populations of their several countries that their Governments are not sentencing them *all* to death, but are prepared to show mercy to a certain percentage. In pursuit of this aim, they advocate fantastic measures which those who invent them must know to be futile. In America, large shelters are advised to be created in all large cities. When the radar chain is completed, it is hoped that there will be 25 minutes' warning of a nuclear attack. When the 25 minute warning is issued, the populations of all the large cities are to rush into the shelters and to stay there until (if ever) it is safe to come out.

I find it quite impossible to believe that those who have devised this fantastic palliative can think that it can serve any useful purpose. Let us consider, stage by stage, what would be likely to happen. Imagine the whole population of (say) New York faced with the prospect of almost certain death if they remained on the surface for another 25 minutes, and officially advised to get into the shelters during this very short time. Everybody knows the sort of thing that happens when a fire in a theatre causes a stampede. If you compare the number of people in a theatre with the number of people in New York, you may get some idea of the stampede which the Authorities recommend. It must be obvious that a very large proportion of those seeking shelters would be trampled to death, and that the only people who would reach the shelters alive would be males muscularly vigorous and morally ruthless. At an optimistic estimate, one might hope that one per cent of the population of New York would reach the shelters undamaged.

### Minimising the danger

How long would they have to stay there? The Authorities speak as if a day or two would be long enough, but they must know that lethal fallout and radioactive soil would make a very much longer stay necessary. Taking the most cheerful view that is at all realistic, let us assume that they are let out after six months because the food in the shelter is, by that time, exhausted. What will they be able to do when they emerge? All food and water will be radioactive. The air they breathe will still be full of Strontium 90. Most will soon die of leukaemia. A few, even more painfully, will die slowly of cancer. The same sort of thing will be happening to the populations of all large cities. The rural population, for whom shelters have not been provided, will already be dead, except for a moribund minority. It must be remembered that roads and railways will have ceased to be usable; most hospitals, medical men and nurses, will have been exterminated; and that the dying population will, in most cases, have to be left without assistance.

There is a tendency on the part of the Authorities to minimise the dangers due to radioactivity and its products. To this there are some honourable, but little advertised, exceptions. For instance, Harwell, the British atomic station, has announced that, in the one year from 1958 to 1959, the amount of Strontium 90 in the bones of British children increased by sixty per cent. Strontium 90 hardly exists in nature and is almost entirely due to nuclear explosions. Since Britain is far removed from any of the test explosions of recent years, it is not likely that the increase of Strontium 90 in British bones is greater than that in bones elsewhere. This makes it highly probably that, throughout the world, those who are not killed quickly in a nuclear war, will die slowly and very painfully of leukaemia of bone cancer.

## Die quietly

The British Government has not hitherto told us much as to what civil defence can do for us. We have been advised that, if our house has no basement, we should die quietly, without making a fuss; but if it has a basement, we should go down into it when we hear the four-minute warning. We should spend four minutes in heaping sand-bags round the walls of the basement to the height of five feet, collecting jars of water and tins of food, and washing and drying the curtains. What remains of the four minutes, we are presumably to spend in repentance. But quite recently the *Daily Mail* has revealed further plans for our salvation. We are to go back beyond the days of the Heptarchy. In those days, England was divided into seven kingdoms, but now it is to be divided into twelve, each with its own Prime Minister. I had thought one Prime Minister bad enough; the thought of twelve appals me. When the four-minute warning sounds, everybody is to dive, simultaneously, into a vast underground refuge, maintaining, one is asked to suppose, perfect order during the descent. There everybody is to stay until the danger of fallout has become small. The *Daily Mail* tells us, cheerfully, that fallout decays rapidly once it is down on the ground. It apparently does not know that, for instance, Strontium 90 has a half-life of 28 years, and Carbon-14, which can cause your children to be idiots or monsters, has a half-life of 5,600 years. The *Daily Mail* report endeavours to persuade us that by these precautions nine-tenths of the population of Great Britain could be saved. I am afraid reality would be rather different. Very many would be killed in the initial panic rush. Others, misled by what they had been told about fallout, would perish soon after emerging. The last few pallid, emaciated stragglers, as they came into something like the light of day, no longer about to shout, would whisper, 'Rule Britannia,' and add themselves to the heap of corpses obstructing the exit. To advocate this sort of thing is called 'patriotism.'

## Why fight and hate?

Is it not obvious that all this is a mad, murderous, monstrous nightmare, imposed upon the world mainly by bands of fanatical lunatics? Why should we think it necessary to fight? Why should we hate the Russians? The Russians offer universal nuclear disarmament, with adequate inspection. They are willing to accept co-existence. The West prefers to invent elaborate schemes of scientific horror. The *Daily Mail*, in the same issue that I have been quoting, reiterates the catchword (as it has become) of Patrick Henry: 'Give me liberty, or give me death.' Patrick Henry did not say, 'Give me liberty, or give everyone death.' This is what his modern imitators say. I am completely at a loss to understand the mentality of those who contemplate, calmly and arithmetically, the immense holocaust that they consider admirable. I cannot but feel that this is the greatest, as it will probably be the last, of the long list of crimes that have darkened the history of our species. What would you think of an individual who, to secure the victory of his own political party, was willing to condemn his own children to an agonising death? What would you think of a man who was willing to extend this cruelty to the whole of the human race? Yet that is what the Governments of the West are doing. And all who have voted for these Governments are accomplices in this immense wickedness. And it is all unnecessary. We only have to let ourselves live in amity and the world could be transformed from a murder factory to a happier community than has ever yet existed.

### Our duty

It is our duty, the duty of those who realise the awful facts, to work with all our power, and with such abilities as we possess, to turn men aside from hate and destruction, to generate such an overwhelming determination to liberate our country and the world from purposeless destruction as shall overcome the stubborn pride of wicked Governments and leave us free to breathe an air uncontaminated by man-made poisons. This is a great task. But, given determination and energy, it can be achieved. As yet we are comparatively few, but we have on our side reason and mercy and the hope of life for coming generations.

**WE CAN WIN, AND WE MUST.**

## Greens stage anti-nuke action

Three MEPs, Molly Scott Cato from the UK, Michèle Rivasi from France, & Tilly Metz from Luxembourg were arrested after breaking into a Belgian military airbase to protest against its stockpiling of American B61 nuclear bombs. The MEPs scaled the perimeter fence and blocked the runway, unfurling a banner which read: "Europe Free of Nuclear weapons." The MEPs were held in a local police station for questioning.

Ahead of the protest, Molly Scott Cato said: "Our action is intended to challenge EU countries to remove US nuclear weapons from European soil. Each B61 bomb is 23 times more powerful than the bomb that devastated Hiroshima. These apocalyptic weapons should find no home in Europe.

"We demand that Europe's nuclear nations immediately sign up to the landmark global Treaty on the Prohibition of Nuclear Weapons and begin the process of decommissioning their nuclear arsenals.

"Nuclear weapons are obsolete in an era of asymmetric warfare and cyber warfare and have no place in a European defence policy for the 21$^{st}$ century. Britain and France have ignored their obligations under the Treaty on the Non-Proliferation of Nuclear Weapons for far too long."

## European Parliament Resolution

The European Parliament agreed a motion for resolution 'on the future of the INF Treaty and the impact on the EU.

There is much in the resolution and although it won a plurality of support within the EP, not everyone will agree with every aspect of it.

However, points 7 and 8 of the resolution are important. They read:

"7. Underlines the urgent need to prevent regional nuclear arms races and the stationing of new nuclear weapons between the Atlantic and the Ural mountains;

8. Commends the entry into force of the UN Treaty on the Prohibition of Nuclear Weapons, the universalisation of the Non-Proliferation Treaty, and the establishment of further nuclear-free zones as positive steps; believes that Europe must lead by example in order to be credible and to advance a nuclear free world to which all European states are committed".

# News from Greece

Europe is at a difficult crossroads on the nuclear issue. The INF Treaty is dead but there is hope, for example, that the TPNW will soon be signed and ratified. So we are happy that the Bertrand Russell Peace Foundation has revived European Nuclear Disarmament – END – to unite once more European people against this deadly threat.

In Greece, though there are no longer any nuclear weapons, the Souda naval base facilitates NATO's ships and submarines carrying nuclear weapons.

Now there is a new danger, if the Insirlic base in Turkey were to close, that the USA nuclear arsenal could be moved to Greece.

As IPPNW and ICAN in Greece we work on three levels: education in schools and public, the media, and meetings with the government.

Using our medical prestige and knowledge, we educate the people about the nuclear danger through lectures in schools, municipalities, cultural unions and through articles.

We remember the history of the Anti-nuclear movement, honour the pioneers like Nikos Nikiforidis and Grigoris Lambrakis, and we use all the anniversaries to create events or publish articles in the press.

In collaboration with others, we use every opportunity to stage major events and to pressurize the government.

We collect signatures from the public in support of the TPNW and from MP's for the Parliamentarian Pledge.

On Hiroshima day in 2017, we managed to add 35 more mayors in Greece, who have joined the "Mayors for Peace" network.

The "Peace Boat" has visited Greece twice and we organised their actions, in order to spread  the message of

Hibakusha testimonies and push for a change of vote at the UN.

In 2015 the representatives of Peace Boat were officially accepted by the president of the Greek Democracy, Mr Pavlopoulos. After ICAN was awarded the Nobel Peace Prize, Mr Pavlopoulos officially congratulated us and underlined the steady commitment of the Greek state against nuclear weapons.

The "Peace Boat" and Hibakusha delegation were accepted three times in the Greek Parliament – 2015, 2017, 2018 – and MP's from all political parties declared their commitment for a nuclear free world.

They were welcomed at the Ministry of Foreign Affairs twice (2105, 2016). The Prime Minister Alexis Tsipras welcomed them at the Maximou Palace on June 6, 2018.

We are in contact with the Cypriot Minister of Foreign Affairs and parliamentarians in order to remind them of the promise they made in Munich last month (February 2019) to ICAN, that they will soon sign TPNW. We are not optimistic for several reasons. On March 22 2019 a meeting was held in Jerusalem between the leaders of Israel, Cyprus and Greece with the presence of the US Foreign Secretary about the protection of oil lines in the region against 'Turkish aggression' and a new US nuclear ship docked at the Suda (Crete) naval base.

We shall use the May 2019 European and Municipality elections to underline the nuclear danger, especially after the end of INF.

On April 22 (Panos Trigazis had the idea) PADOP will for the first time award the 'NN Medal' (Nikos Nikiforidis – Non Nuclear) to people who work for nuclear abolition.

Though we are not optimistic about a change of policy in Greece for our cause, we will keep reminding people of the lethal and urgent danger of the nuclear threat and push any government and all political parties to gain their commitment for a nuclear free world, whilst hoping that there will be a better political moment in future.

There is always hope. When we all started to fight for the NPT and the other anti-nuclear Treaties, the political climate was worse, but we won. The urgent elimination of nuclear weapons is the only cure for this disease that threatens all humanity.

*Maria Arvaniti Sotiropoulou*
President of the Greek Affiliate
Representative of ICAN in Greece

# Enough spending on nuclear weapons!
## *News from France*

Mouvement de la Paix, a French non-governmental organization founded in 1948 is dedicated to promoting peace, opposing wars and nuclear weapons. It reiterates its opposition to the military programming law 2019-2025, which devotes 295 billion to an increase in the military budget. Concretely, from 34 billion to 44 billion per year, it brings this expenditure to 2% of France's GDP (which is of 2,200 billions), the highest increase in military spending. This represents an increase from 8.5% to more than 11.3% of the state budget (386 Billion/year). This is no less than 37 billion for the modernisation of the French nuclear force by 2025. "The cost of nuclear deterrence will double to 6 billion euros per year by 2030".

By modernizing its weapons and dedicating such an increase in its budget, France loses its credibility to prevent other countries from gaining access to nuclear weapons. These nuclear weapons are illegal, dangerous, costly, militarily useless and ethically unacceptable. All other weapons of mass destruction are prohibited. There is an urgent need to ratify the treaty banning nuclear weapons, which was voted in July 2017 at the United Nations.

Enough spending on these weapons of mass destruction! Mouvement de la Paix is strongly involved in the campaign against nuclear weapons, for instance by its participation in the celebration of the International Day of Peace 21 September. It is also "fighting" against militarization of space and against the arms trade with in particular the mobilizations against the Eurosatory exhibition, held every tow years in June in Paris Villepinte.

What an honnor for France if this country would renounce modernizing its nuclear arsenal and to commit itself to disarmament!

*Patrice Salzenstein*
Mouvement de la Paix, France

● ● ● ● ● ● ● ● ● ● ● ● ● ● ● ● ● ● ●

# Towards a nuclear weapons free Europe:
## *European Green Party Resolution*

Between 23 and 25 November 2018, the European Green Party convened in Berlin for their Council meeting. At this Council, the EGP adopted a resolution titled 'Towards a nuclear weapons free Europe'.

The resolution opens: "American nuclear weapons still linger on European Union soil ... The presence of the American nuclear weapons in Europe, the Russian nuclear weapons and means of delivery in the Western part of their country and continued investments in British and French nuclear arsenals is inconsistent with the

EGP's peace policy ... The establishment of a European nuclear-weapons free zone, the perspective of nuclear disarmament in Europe and EU28 joining the TPNW should be included in current discussions about the EU's security and defence policy. The EU should lead by example and make concrete steps towards nuclear disarmament of the continent."

See vote.europeangreens.eu for more information.

● ● ● ● ● ● ● ● ● ● ● ● ● ● ● ● ● ● ● ●

# INF Treaty at threat: Prevent a 21ˢᵗ century nuclear arms race
## *IPB Statement*

On February 2nd, President Trump announced the unilateral suspension of the US from the Intermediate-Range Nuclear Forces (INF) Treaty. After several months of verbal escalation, the United States rejected the Russian offer to inspect a suspected missile (Novator 9M729) and declared that it would announce its decision on February 2nd.

Russia accused the United States of violating the Treaty by deploying a component of a missile defence system – the Mark 41 Vertical Launch System (VLS) – that is capable of launching offensive missiles.

By suspending its compliance with the Treaty, the United States will then be able to deploy prohibited missiles in Europe. In reaction of the unlawful behaviour of the US, Russia withdrew from the treaty as a reaction to the US actions. These attacks against this significant nuclear arms treaty are almost inevitably setting off a new arms race. Meanwhile, the US is renewing the nuclear weapons based in five European countries.

The INF treaty led to the elimination and renunciation of deployments of all US and Russian nuclear and conventional ground-launched cruise

and ballistic missiles with ranges of 500 to 5,000 km. Signed in 1987, after millions of people had fought to stop the nuclear arms race, it has dramatically reduced the danger of Europe becoming the primary theatre for a nuclear war and thus marked the end of the Cold War.

IPB calls for a massive and united mobilization of all the forces opposed to this project of mass destruction to work together, nationally and internationally, to avert a new nuclear arms race.

We urgently appeal for negotiations to preserve and reinforce the INF Treaty and associate all other nuclear-armed states. In addition, NATO governments are called upon to take a clear stance of against the usage of Intermediate-Range Nuclear Forces and support bilateral and international negotiations. The global population depends on a new coalition of sensibility and reasonability.

IPB calls on all countries to ratify the Treaty on the Prohibition of Nuclear Weapons, adopted by the UN in 2017, which offers a solid international framework for the elimination of nuclear weapons.

With peaceful wishes,
Reiner Braun & Lisa Clark
Co-Presidents of the
International Peace Bureau

# Keys to Armageddon
*"You have my permission to fire"*

With this simple phrase, 16 nuclear-armed Polaris missiles, each of which was 30 times as powerful as the Hiroshima bomb, could have been launched into the stratosphere on a free-fall path to targets in the former Soviet Union. Their use would have marked the end of the world as we know it; an act of retaliation for the launch of similar nuclear weapons by the Soviet Union at Britain or her NATO partners under the policy of mutually assured destruction. It would have caused a nuclear winter akin to the one that wiped the dinosaurs off the planet. It would have been an act too dreadful for any reasonable person to contemplate for long.

Except that we did. As executive officer of a Polaris submarine in the mid-1970s, I took part in multiple exercises intended to prepare us to launch our missiles in a nuclear confrontation. In the event of a real one I would have been party to authenticating that the order to fire came from the prime minister. I would have been required to stand next to the captain as he inserted his dedicated key in the firing panel and turned it to complete the electronic circuits that would then irrevocably count down to the launch of the first missile. It would have been an unimaginable moment.

It is a matter of history that this

never happened for real during the cold war. It is a matter of policy, however, that it still could – for the UK, the US and at least four other countries that maintain a submarine-based nuclear deterrent ...

My captain and I had our own private and very serious discussions before we went on patrol together for the first time. We both wanted to be quite clear that we were of the same mind about how we would respond if we received an order to fire. We agreed that we could not obey an unlawful order just because it came with the authority of the prime minister.

This view was based on recent history. The Nuremberg Principles established after the Second World War that "the fact that a person acted pursuant to order of his Government or of a superior does not relieve him from responsibility under international law, provided a moral choice was in fact possible to him".

Our dilemma was that the use of nuclear weapons by any yardstick had to be an offence against prevailing humanitarian law as expressed in the Geneva Conventions ...

The question, then, was what would constitute a lawful order to fire ... my captain and I agreed that, if the UK or NATO was subjected to a nuclear attack, then the norms of humanitarian law no longer applied and we would fire as ordered. In these terrible circumstances the hope, possibly vain, would be to halt further nuclear exchanges.

What we were not prepared to do under any circumstance was automatically obey an order to fire first with the intention of destroying Soviet targets before they fired at us. This would almost certainly have been unlawful (and arguably still would be) and neither of us had any wish to start a nuclear war ...

*Commander Robert Forsyth RN (Ret'd)*

The full version of this article can be found at: tinyurl.com/y3kuswma. Commander Forsyth has given important evidence to an ongoing UK Parliamentary Inquiry into authorising military action. See *ENDINFO 2* for further information.

● ● ● ● ● ● ● ● ● ● ● ● ● ● ● ● ● ● ● ● ● ●

# New Arms Race

Twenty years after the end of the Cold War, a new nuclear arms race between the USA and Russia looms over Europe, following the disengagement of presidents Trump and Putin from the historic INF Treaty of 1987.

Greece has very painful experiences from that dark period of the 20th century, as its northern borders were the dividing East-West line in the Balkan region. As a result, the Greece peace and anti-nuclear movement from the outset supported the idea for a nuclear weapon free Balkans and for a nuclear weapon free Europe from the Atlantic to the Urals.

We do not forget that the opposition to "euro missiles" generated one of the greatest peace movements, especially in Western Europe and END (European Nuclear Disarmament) played a decisive role towards this development.

At that time, I was general secretary of the Greece Peace Committee (EEDYE) belonging to the WPC, but this did not prevent us from joining successive END conferences. In addition, "no to euro missiles" was an issue that brought together the three main national peace organisations, AKE, EEDYE and KEADEA. So, we

may say that it is time to repeat the unitary actions of that era.

PADOP has already published the new END Appeal, which has inspired me personally to write an article for daily newspapers in Athens. In addition, we plan a special event within the framework of the forthcoming monthly campaign on disarmament and reducing globally military spending.

The INF was significant for Europe and the victorious antinuclear movement of the 1980s, "the most dangerous decade", according to our great friend Ken Coates.

Warm congratulations to those who took the initiative to revive END!

Panos Trigazis
PADOP President, Greece

● ● ● ● ● ● ● ● ● ● ● ● ● ● ● ● ● ● ● ● ● ●

# Luciana Castellina awarded peace prize

Luciana Castellina, former MEP (and now a candidate in Greece), reporter and peace activist has been awarded the inaugural Nikos Nikiforidis Prize for her work as a founder of European Nuclear Disarmament in the 1980s.

Castellina played a central role in developing the movement and worked closedly with Ken Coates, from the Bertrand Russell Peace Foundation. Her support and ongoing contribution to European Nuclear Disarmament has been recognized in the awarding of this prize named after a 22 year old martyr of the anti-nuclear movement.

Nikiforidis was executed in 1951 in Thessaloniki because he was collecting signatures for the Stockholm Appeal. The International Peace Buraeu selected him to be among the people who should be honored internationally for their work for peace.

• • • • • • • • • • • • • • • • • • • • • •

# Two thirds of Belgians favour banning nukes

**LE SOIR**

Nucléaire: 64 % des Belges favorables au désarmement

Two-thirds of Belgians want the country to countersign the banning of nuclear weapons, according to an opinion poll conducted by the Belgian coalition against atomic weaponry.

In 2017, 122 member states of the UN voted in favour of banning nuclear weapons. The treaty aims to halt the development, testing, production, stockpiling, trade in, use and the threat to use nuclear arms. This is not the case in Belgium or NATO's other member states.

The majority of those taking part in the poll (66%) were also in favour of the withdrawal of Belgian financial institutions from the nuclear armaments industry.

The majority (53%) also considers that the new F35 fighter jets should not have a nuclear capacity, which is about double the number of those who said they were in favour (27%).

Those polled who said they were against the presence of American nuclear weapons at Kleine Brogel are also more numerous than those declaring themselves in favour of maintaining it (49% against 27%).

The Belgian coalition against atomic weapons, therefore, wants the different political parties to take these results into account before the next elections.

[source: *Brussels Times*]

• • • • • • • • • • • • • • • • • • • • • •

# Armed to the teeth

(Stockholm, 29 April 2019) Total world military expenditure rose to $1822 billion in 2018, representing an increase of 2.6 per cent from 2017, according to new data from the Stockholm International Peace Research Institute (SIPRI). The five biggest spenders in

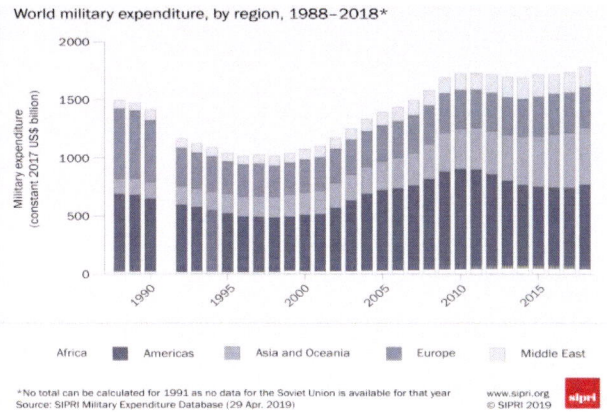

World military expenditure, by region, 1988–2018*

Africa    Americas    Asia and Oceania    Europe    Middle East

*No total can be calculated for 1991 as no data for the Soviet Union is available for that year
Source: SIPRI Military Expenditure Database (29 Apr. 2019)

www.sipri.org
© SIPRI 2019

Total global military spending rose for the second consecutive year in 2018, to the highest level since 1988 –the first year for which consistent global data is available. World spending is now 76 per cent higher than the post-cold war low in 1998. World military spending in 2018 represented 2.1 per cent of global gross domestic product (GDP) or $239 per person. 'In 2018 the USA and China accounted for half of the world's military spending,' says Dr Nan Tian, a researcher with the SIPRI Arms and Military Expenditure (AMEX) programme. 'The higher level of world military expenditure in 2018 is mainly the result of significant increases in spending by these two countries.'

2018 were the United States, China, Saudi Arabia, India and France, which together accounted for 60 per cent of global military spending. Military spending by the USA increased for the first time since 2010, while spending by China grew for the 24th consecutive year. The comprehensive annual update of the SIPRI Military Expenditure Database is now accessible at www.sipri.org.

END INFO

For more info or to subscribe, contact:
tomunterrainer@russfound.org

# *International Meeting*
# NUCLEAR SECURITY IN EUROPE
## AFTER THE COLLAPSE OF THE INF

# September 14th, 2019 Brussels
## 11am to 5pm, venue tba

Tensions are growing among states possessing nuclear weapons and the collapse of the Intermediate-range Nuclear Forces (INF) Treaty brings Europe closer to the brink of another dangerous Cold War. Meanwhile, the UN Treaty on the Prohibition of Nuclear Weapons (TPNW) gains traction and opens new avenues for urgently needed common campaigns and actions.

> Peace groups ... International peace networks ... Social and environmental movements ... Churches ... Trade unions ... Everyone who wants to make the planet safer ... All are welcome to discuss this challenging situation and the way forward to a nuclear-weapons-free Europe.

Signed in 1987 by the Unites States and the Soviet Union, the INF Treaty bans a complete class of nuclear weapons -- land-based cruise and ballistic missiles with ranges of 500 to 5,500km. The Treaty signalled a victory on the part of millions of Europeans who, during the 1980s, demonstrated against the "Euromissiles". As the United States and Russia again spend enormous sums on modernizing their nuclear arsenals, tensions between both countries are widely recognized as being at their worst since the end of the Cold War.

How do we stop this nuclear arms race? How best to promote and implement the Treaty on the Prohibition of Nuclear Weapons? What alternatives are there for peace and common/human security in Europe? How can we achieve European Nuclear Disarmament?

A detailed agenda will be published in July. Please save the date and if you are interested in attending, please send a note to info@ipb.org. Feel free to share this invitation!

Called by: INTERNATIONAL PEACE BUREAU – BERTRAND RUSSELL PEACE FOUNDATION – PAX CHRISTI – A2000/EUROPE NUCLEAR WEAPONS WORKING GROUP – INTERNATIONAL NETWORK OF ENGINEERS AND SCIENTISTS FOR GLOBAL RESPONSIBILITY – INTERNATIONAL PHYSICIANS FOR THE PREVENTION OF NUCLEAR WAR – INTERNATIONAL TRADE UNION CONFEDERATION

With the support of TRANSFORM

# Our house is on fire

*Greta Thunberg*

*Greta is a 16-year-old Swedish climate activist. She initiated the 'School Strike for Climate' movement, which saw 1.4 million students around the world take action on 15 March 2019. She spoke at Davos in January 2019.*

Our house is on fire, I am here to say our house is on fire. According to the Intergovernmental Panel on Climate Change we are less than 12 years away from not being able to undo our mistakes.

In that time unprecedented changes in all aspects of society need to have taken place, including a reduction of our $CO_2$ emissions by at least 50%. Please note that those numbers do not include the aspect of equity which is absolutely necessary to make the Paris agreement work on a global scale. Nor does it include tipping points or feedback loops like the extreme, powerful methane gas being released from the thawing Arctic permafrost.

At places like Davos people like to tell success stories, but their financial success has come with an unthinkable price tag. And on climate change we have to acknowledge that we have failed. All political movements in their present form have done so. And the media has failed to create broad public awareness. But *Homo sapiens* has not yet failed. Yes we are failing but there is still time to turn everything around. We can still fix this, we still have everything in our own hands. But unless we recognize the overall failures of our current systems we probably don't stand a chance.

We are facing a disaster of unspoken sufferings for enormous amounts of people and now is not the time for speaking politely, focusing on what we can or cannot say. Now it's the time to speak clearly. Solving the climate crisis is the greatest and most complex challenge that *Homo sapiens* has have ever faced.

The main solution, however, is so simple that even a small child can understand it.

We have to stop the emissions of greenhouse gases. And either we do that or we don't. You say nothing in life is black or white but that is a lie, a very dangerous lie. Either we prevent a 1.5 degree warming or we don't. Either we avoid setting off that irreversible chain reaction beyond human control, or we don't. Either we choose to go on as a civilization or we don't. That is as black or white as it gets.

There are no grey areas when it comes to survival. Now we all have a choice. We can create transformational action that will safeguard the future living conditions for humankind, or we can continue with our business as usual and fail. That is up to you and me.

Some say that we should not engage in activism, instead we should leave everything to our politicians and just vote for change instead. But what do we do when there is no political will? What do we do when the politics needed are nowhere in sight?

Here in Davos, just like everywhere else, everyone is talking about money. It seems that money and growth are our only main concerns. And since the climate crisis is a crisis that has never once been treated as a crisis, people are simply not aware of the full consequences for our everyday life.

People are not aware that there is such a thing as a carbon budget, and just how incredibly small that remaining carbon budget is. And that needs to change today. No other current challenge can match the importance of establishing a wide public awareness and understanding of our rapidly disappearing carbon budgets, that should and must become a new global currency in the very heart of future and present economics.

We are now at a time in history where everyone with any insight into the climate crisis that threatens our civilization and the entire biosphere must speak out in clear language, no matter how uncomfortable and unprofitable that may be. We must change almost everything in our current societies. The bigger your carbon footprint is, the bigger your moral duty. The bigger your platform the bigger your responsibility.

Adults keep saying we owe it to the young people to give them hope. But I don't want your hope, I don't want you to be hopeful. I want you to panic, I want you to feel the fear I feel every day. And then I want you to act, I want you to act as if you would in a crisis. I want you to act as if the house was on fire, because it is.

# Julian Assange – Nobel Prize?

*Mairead Maguire*

*The author and Betty Williams were awarded the Nobel Peace Prize in 1976 for building a movement called the 'Peace People' that would play a part in helping to move the communities of Northern Ireland towards a peace process and, eventually, the Good Friday Agreement of 1998. Now, Mairead has requested permission from the UK Home Office to visit her friend Julian Assange in prison. She has nominated him for the Nobel Peace Prize.*

I want to visit Julian to see he is receiving medical care and to let him know that there are many people around the world who admire him and are grateful for his courage in trying to stop the wars and end the suffering of others.

Thursday 11th April 2019 will go down in history as a dark day for the rights of humanity when Julian Assange, a brave and good man, was arrested by the British Metropolitan Police, forcibly removed without prior warning, in a style befitting a war criminal, from the Ecuadorian Embassy, and bundled into a police van. It is a sad time when the UK Government, at the behest of the United States Government, arrested Julian Assange, a symbol of freedom of speech as the publisher of Wikileaks. The world's leaders and mainstream media remain silent on the fact that he is an innocent man until proven guilty, while the UN Working Group on Arbitrary Detention defines him as innocent. The decision of President Lenin Moreno of Ecuador who, under financial pressure from the United States, has withdrawn asylum to the Wikileaks founder, is a further example of the US's global currency monopoly, pressurizing other countries to do their bidding or face the financial and possibly violent consequences for disobedience to the alleged world Super Power, which has sadly lost its moral compass.

Julian Assange had taken asylum in the Ecuadorian Embassy seven years ago precisely because he foresaw that the US would demand his extradition to face a Grand Jury for mass murders carried out not by him but by US and NATO forces, and concealed from the public.

Unfortunately, it is my belief that Julian Assange will not see a fair trial. As we have seen over the last seven years, time and time again, the European countries and many others do not have the political will or clout to stand up for what they know is right, and will eventually cave into the Unites States' will. We have watched Chelsea Manning being returned to jail and to solitary confinement, so we must not be naive in our thinking: surely, this is the future for Julian Assange.

I visited Julian on two occasions in the Ecuadorian Embassy and was very impressed with this courageous and highly intelligent man. The first visit was on my return from Kabul, where young Afghan teenage boys insisted on writing a letter with the request I carry it to Julian Assange, to thank him for publishing on Wikileaks the truth about the war in Afghanistan and to help stop their homeland being bombed by planes and drones. All had a story of brothers or friends killed by drones while collecting wood in winter on the mountains.

On 8 January 2019, I nominated Julian Assange for the Nobel Peace Prize. I issued a press release hoping to bring attention to his nomination, which seemed to have been widely ignored by Western media. By Julian's courageous actions, and others like him, we could see full well the atrocities of war. The release of the files brought to our doors the atrocities our governments carried out. It is my strong belief that this is the true essence of an activist and it is my great shame I live in an era when people like Julian Assange, Edward Snowden, Chelsea Manning and anyone willing to open our eyes to the atrocities of war is likely to be hunted like an animal by governments, punished and silenced. Therefore, I believe the British government should oppose the extradition of Assange as it sets a dangerous precedent for journalists, whistleblowers and other sources of truth the US may wish to pressure in the future. This man is paying a high price to end war and for peace and non-violence, and we should all remember that.

\* \* \*

***Julian Assange*** *has been awarded the 2019 European United Left-Nordic Green Left Award for Journalists, Whistleblowers and Defenders of the Right to Information, WikiLeaks reported in April.*

The award is given to individuals 'uncovering the truth and exposing it to the public' and to honour 'individuals or groups who have been intimidated and/or persecuted' for such actions. It thus recognizes Assange's work through WikiLeaks.

The prize is sponsored by European left-wing parliamentarians, who devised it in 2018 in honour of assassinated Maltese journalist **Daphne Galizia**. Nobel Peace prize winner (1976), **Mairead Maguire,** received it on Assange's behalf at an event in the European Parliament in Strasbourg.

Assange is a prize winning journalist with more than 15 international awards for his work, including the 2008 New Media Award from *The Economist*, 2010 *Time* Person of the Year (Readers' Choice), and the 2009 Amnesty International UK Media Award. His defence lawyers have repeatedly explained that, by being a publisher and journalist, US imprisonment would mean the violation of his fundamental right to freedom of expression.

'The warning is explicit towards journalists. What happened to the founder and editor of WikiLeaks can happen to you in a newspaper, you in a TV studio, you on the radio, you running a podcast,' said award-winning journalist **John Pilger,** writing an op-ed for teleSUR.

On 11 April 2019, Assange's seven-year asylum was abruptly removed and he was arrested by British police. Immediately, the US charged him with a 'computer hacking conspiracy', over an allegation he conspired with former army intelligence analyst Chelsea Manning to break into a classified government computer.

*www.peacepeople.com*

# Citizen Denied

*Emma DeSouza*

*Emma DeSouza and her American husband are into the fifth year of their long struggle to assert their right to family life in Northern Ireland. In her recent open letter to the UK Home Secretary, as yet unanswered, Emma sets out how the UK government takes an increasingly hard line, contrary to the terms of the Good Friday Agreement, in denying rights to Irish nationals in the North. Although an EU and Irish citizen, she has less rights than her counterparts in the Republic of Ireland.*

To The Rt Hon. Sajid Javid,
Secretary of State for the Home Office

The Good Friday Agreement is widely championed as a success — revered as a model of peace and celebrated worldwide. Yet your department has openly disregarded the Agreement, and is actively seeking to undermine its very foundation. The people of Northern Ireland are unique within the United Kingdom in that we have the birthright to identify and be accepted as Irish or British or both — a right enshrined in the international treaty your government claims to be upholding through the Brexit negotiations. Contrary to the statutory duty on your department to accept the birthright provisions of the Good Friday Agreement, your department is arguing through the British courts that the people of Northern Ireland are 'automatically British' as we were 'clearly born in the United Kingdom'. Your department regularly and repeatedly forces British citizenship on Irish citizens born in Northern Ireland — citizens who are Irish by birth and by choice — a choice the people of this island voted for overwhelmingly in the Good Friday Agreement referendum — a choice you and your department are denying.

I am an Irish national born in Northern Ireland, who has spent the last four years in legal proceedings at the hands of your department. The position of the Home Office is that I'm a dual British/Irish national due to my birth in Northern Ireland, and if I would like to fully retain and access my rights as an Irish/EU national in the United Kingdom, I am 'welcome to renounce my British citizenship and rely on my Irish citizenship'.

I have never claimed British citizenship and do not hold a British passport.

It's difficult to understand your personal view or commitment to the integrity of the Good Friday Agreement, as you are not on record on the subject, and have to date ignored all correspondence from myself and senior political figures on this issue. We only have the court documents lodged by your department to guide us on the view of the Home Office and British government. The position, according to these documents, is that the people of Northern Ireland are 'as a matter of law British', with the counterintuitive argument that there 'is nothing in the Belfast Agreement to prevent British citizenship being acquired at birth'. Further, the documents troublingly elaborate – 'A treaty HMG is a party of does not alter the laws of the United Kingdom' and that the 'courts do not have the power to force the government to uphold its obligations and commitments to a treaty'. These arguments have been reaffirmed by the Immigration Minister, Caroline Nokes, who stated 'Our view is that an international agreement such as the Belfast Good Friday Agreement cannot supersede domestic legislation'.

Legally, treaties are to be interpreted in good faith and in accordance with the meaning given to the terms within them, in light of their context and purpose. The motivation for your department's refusal to accept that the Good Friday Agreement is a UN-registered international treaty between two sovereign states, and that the government is expected to act in accordance with said treaty, remains unclear. What is clear, however, is that an Irish identity in Northern Ireland comes at great personal cost. It could be losing your right to work. It could be losing your right to travel. It could be losing the right to say a final goodbye to a loved one before they're gone. It could be all of these things, or it could be something else entirely. NI citizens are losing their right to be who they are.

I, as well as many others, have had to stand in court detailing every moment of our lives where our Irish identity was evident, at the behest of your department. We are being asked to literally prove that we are Irish.

Prime Minister Theresa May acknowledged that an incompatibility between Home Office policies and commitments to the Good Friday Agreement exists. An urgent review was promised in order to bring policy 'in line with the letter and spirit of the Good Friday Agreement'. In response to a Freedom of Information request, we have since discovered that there is no formal review, no progress, and no terms of reference or timeframe held on record. Instead of a solution to the detrimental treatment of Irish citizens in Northern Ireland, we are seeing a hardening of the British Home Office position. At every opportunity the principles of the

Good Friday Agreement are being reneged on.

Under recent policy changes, NI-born Irish citizens will be unable to fully retain and access their EU rights and entitlements within the United Kingdom. The EU Settlement Scheme is the British government's enactment of the citizens' rights chapter of the Withdrawal Agreement. It remains open to Irish citizens born in the Republic of Ireland, whilst it is closed to Irish citizens born in Northern Ireland. This is creating a two tier system for Irish citizens: those who can fully retain their EU rights and benefits under the Settlement Scheme, and those who cannot. Whilst it is noted that the Home Office has advised Irish citizens that they 'do not need to apply but can do so if they wish', is also important to note that their non Irish/British family members need to apply. The Common Travel Area is cited as a reason for Irish citizens to not apply under the scheme but it remains largely unimplemented and unenforceable. The restrictions on NI born Irish citizens will result in a loss of wider EU rights, such as Family Reunification. We will be among the only EU citizens within the United Kingdom to face such a restriction. How can the Home Secretary justify the marginalisation of one group of Irish citizens?

I ask you, as Home Secretary, to consider the will of the people of this island. We voted for peace and the recognition of the unique status of Northern Ireland. There is no equality in legally allowing NI-born citizens to be exclusively British whilst denying that same right to those who wish to be Irish. No citizen should have their identity questioned or be instructed to renounce any citizenship in order to access an entitlement.

There is an onus on you, as Home Secretary, to take responsibility for the derogation of duties to the Belfast Good Friday Agreement, and to the people of Northern Ireland. I ask that you outline how your department will address and rectify the clear incompatibility between Home Office policies and the Good Friday Agreement.

To the British government – we have waited, and we have waited patiently, for the full implementation of the Good Friday Agreement and full realization of our rights. In the face of Brexit we cannot wait any longer. It is time for the Good Friday Agreement to become what it was destined to be. I ask that the British Government implements the Good Friday Agreement in all its parts.

*Emma DeSouza*

**PERMANENT EUROPEAN UNION CITIZENSHIP**
EUROPEAN CITIZENS' INITIATIVE
www.eucitizen2017.org I Facebook /eucitizen2017 I Twitter @EUCitizen2017

## Permanent European Union Citizenship

### European Citizens' Initiative

EU citizens elect the European Parliament and participate in its work, thus exercising treaty rights, enhancing Union democracy, and reinforcing its citizenship. Noting the ECJ's view of Union citizenship as a 'fundamental status' of nationals of Member States, and that Brexit will strip millions of EU citizens of this status and their vote in European elections, requests the Commission propose means to avoid risk of collective loss of EU citizenship and rights, and assure all EU citizens that, once attained, such status is permanent and their rights acquired.

*To endorse the Permanent EU Citizenship ECI,*
*follow the link at www.eucitizen2017.org*

# Jo Vellacott

## 1922-2019

Jo Vellacott, who died in February in Toronto aged 96, was a pioneer in the study of women's history, drawing particular attention to the intersection between the National Union of Women's Suffrage Societies and resistance to the First World War.

Born in Plymouth, Devon, Jo was the youngest of the three children of Harold Vellacott, a surgeon, and Josephine (née Semphill), a nurse. She boarded at Downe House school in Berkshire where a formative influence was Quaker history teacher, Jean Rowntree. On graduating from Oxford University in 1943, Jo worked as an aircraft mechanic in the Women's Royal Naval Service during the Second World War.

After the war, Jo applied for work through the intriguingly titled 'Society for the Overseas Settlement of British Women' and was appointed to teach English in South Africa. There she met Peter Newberry, a medical student who had been a South African Air Force pilot. They married in 1949 and moved in 1953 to the UK, before emigrating in 1955, with their three children, to Canada when Peter was appointed as a medic in the Canadian Air Force. Moving with Peter's various postings, Jo combined family life with employment as a schoolteacher and as a lecturer in history and women's studies at different universities as the family moved around the country, living in Ottawa, the Yukon, Edmonton, London (Ontario) and Toronto. She gained a history PhD from McMaster University in Hamilton, Ontario, in 1978.

Although Jo lived in Canada for the rest of her life, her work on the early pacifist activism of Bertrand Russell brought her back to the UK on grant-funded research projects from the 1960s, and led to a rediscovery of the role of the Edwardian feminist and First World War pacifist Catherine Marshall. She had hoped to trace the long lost (and still lost) archives of the No Conscription Fellowship (NCF) but instead was pointed to an unsorted hoard of papers at County Archives in Carlisle Castle. They had been recently rescued from a dilapidated shed in the grounds of an outdoor activity centre near Keswick and were known to include correspondence with Russell and many other leading academics, activists and politicians of the early 20th century. The papers had belonged to the previous owner of the property, Catherine Marshall, who had died almost unknown, in 1961. As Jo discovered, they contained unique records of Marshall's work with the NCF and her earlier pivotal role in the National Union of Women's Suffrage Societies (NUWSS). Jo's work on Russell and Marshall coincided with a 1960s resurgence of the peace movement in Britain and a focus on women's history that accompanied 'second wave' feminism. It inspired radical alternative perspectives to the conventional narrative about how the vote for women was won and on women's responses to war, challenging the idea that suffragists and suffragettes alike had overwhelmingly backed the war effort.

Jo's first book, *Bertrand Russell and the Pacifists in the First World War* (1981), and her biography of Marshall, *From Liberal to Labour with Women's Suffrage: The Story of Catherine Marshall* (1993), were both reissued in new editions by Spokesman to mark the centenary of the First World War. Her analysis of the way anti-war suffragism played out from 1914 is most evident in *Pacifists, Patriots and the Vote: The erosion of democratic suffragism* (2007). The effect of an 'Election Fighting Fund', established from 1912, was that NUWSS funds and organisational support would be given to Labour candidates at the general election due in 1915, in any constituency where the incumbent and/or other candidates of the main (Liberal and Conservative) parties did not pledge support for a women's suffrage measure. As coordinator of the Fund and Parliamentary Secretary of the NUWSS, Catherine Marshall lobbied MPs, party leaders and government ministers as to possible consequences for their political ambitions. Had there been an election in 1915 it is likely that a pro-suffrage House of Commons would have passed a more comprehensive Act than that of 1918. The NUWSS had a growing mass membership, a more democratic structure, a wider feminist agenda, and more working class support and inclusion than the much smaller Women's Social and Political Union (WSPU — suffragettes). In 1915, the NUWSS split over support for the war. 'Pacifist' and internationalist members of the National Committee were a majority but all resigned leaving a more conservative and 'patriotic' faction, led by Millicent Fawcett, in charge. Jo found evidence that NUWSS archives had later been 'weeded' to misrepresent the schism and minimise the contribution of Marshall and others to the pre-war NUWSS campaigns. From the evidence of his own correspondence, Marshall had been personally instrumental in recruiting Russell to the No Conscription Fellowship

*Jo Vellacott on her last visit to Britain*

cause early in 1916. Jo reveals, in fascinating and forensic detail, the often strained but essential collaboration between them in sustaining the NCF while its younger male leaders, including co-founders Fenner Brockway and Clifford Allen, were imprisoned. Without the illumination of Jo's work, convergent trends between feminism and socialism on the eve of war and the role of women war-resisters after 1914 had been seriously neglected.

A tangible recent outcome is that Catherine Marshall's name and portrait are engraved, with those of other suffragists, on the plinth of Millicent Fawcett's statue, unveiled in Parliament Square, London, in 2018. And a blue plaque commemorating Marshall was unveiled in October that year at her former home at Hawse End near Keswick. Jo was unable to travel by then but contributed an enthusiastic and moving message of greeting that was read on the occasion (see *Spokesman 141*).

As a relative of Catherine Marshall and history teacher, I was fortunate to meet Jo several times on her later visits to Britain. I am grateful for her work in highlighting Catherine, a largely forgotten heroine of first-wave feminism and war resistance who had died long before I knew of her. In person Jo was unfailingly generous and patient in her support for those who shared her wide interests and determined in her conscientious pursuit of truth. A commitment to progressive ideals infuses her writing without distracting from rigorous attention to detail in presenting evidence and evaluating its sources. Humane insights with a spirit of tolerance and compassion can be found even when her protagonists least appear to deserve it. Her intellect was undimmed by declining energy in the last months of her illness with pancreatic cancer.

Jo, who became a Quaker in her 40s, was able to complete a fascinating account of her own early life, *Living and Learning in Peace and War*, published by Spokesman in 2017. She would have wished to complete a second volume of her biography of Marshall (the first takes her story only to the outbreak of World War One) but this task has been left to Lyndsey Jenkins with a comprehensive foundation of notes and drafts that Jo has passed on.

Jo's marriage to Peter ended in divorce in 1979. She is survived by their children, Mary, Soo and Douglas, five grandchildren and two great-grandchildren.

*Simon Colbeck*

*Catherine Marshall on the plinth of Millicent Fawcett's statue*

# Spokesman Books: Jo Vellacott Titles

## Conscientious Objection:
### Bertrand Russell and the Pacifists in the First World War

This story of the No-Conscription Fellowship (NCF) focuses on Bertrand Russell's contribution, it has been recognised as contributing to an understanding of how the NCF was made up, how it worked, its successes and failures, and dissensions within it, particularly over the acceptability of various forms of alternative service and of political action in the cause of peace.

Price: £14.99 | 340 pages | Paperback | ISBN: 978 0 85124 8424

## From Liberal to Labour with Women's Suffrage *The Story of Catherine Marshall*

Catherine Marshall was a vital figure in the women's suffrage movement in Britain before the First World War. Using her remarkable political skills on behalf of the major non-militant organization, the National Union of Women's Suffrage Societies, she built close connections with major suffragist politicians, leading some - in all three parties - to consider adopting a measure of women's enfranchisement as a party plank.

Price: £17.99 | 518 pages | Paperback | ISBN: 978 0 85124 8523

## Living and Learning in Peace and War

This is a memoir of the first twenty-five years of a long life. Jo Vellacott's early years were lived under the shadow still cast by the First World War, but at a time when it was still possible to hope that it had indeed been the war to end all wars. Gradually the skies darkened and the rise of Nazism came to threaten the world.

Price: £10.99 | 190 pages | Paperback | ISBN: 978 0 85124 8707

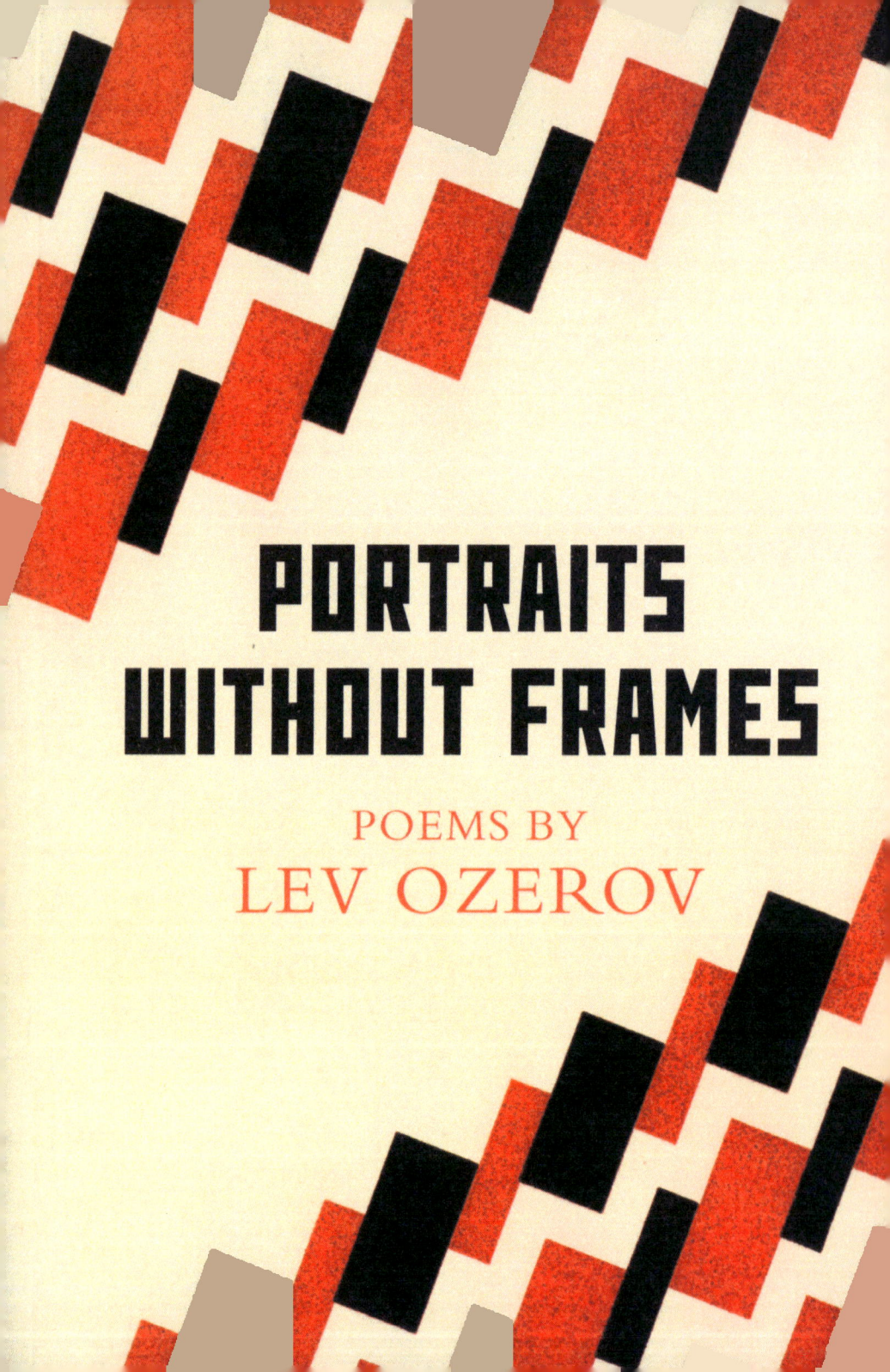

# PORTRAITS WITHOUT FRAMES

POEMS BY
## LEV OZEROV

ANDREY PLATONOV (1899–1951) is one of the greatest of all Russian writers. His longer works were published only many years after his death, but the short stories he published during his lifetime are no less remarkable. "Fro" is one of the most charming and tender of these. Most of Platonov's best short stories and short novels have been translated by Robert and Elizabeth Chandler, in collaboration with Olga Meerson and other translators.

## ANDREY PLATONOVICH PLATONOV

Platonov is reading aloud,
reading "Fro"
in the spacious apartment of Kornely
Lyutsianovich Zelinsky,*
just by the Moscow Art Theater.
"A grand little hut!"
he said afterwards,
without a trace of envy.

Platonov reads with animation.
I had not heard of Platonov.
I know nothing of his ways,
of his way in life.
"That's splendid!" I blurt out,
unable to contain myself,
when he reads the last page.
Piercing eyes,
and on his lips—kindness
and irony, irony

*Zelinsky was a Soviet literary critic of great influence from the early 1930s until his death. In 1940 he wrote a damning internal review of a collection of poems that Marina Tsvetaeva, recently returned to the Soviet Union, was trying to publish. He also played an important part in the public attacks on Boris Pasternak in 1958, after *Doctor Zhivago* had been published abroad.

◀ See Reviews page 101

and kindness. Wary,
Platonov says nothing.
"Yes, but hardly relevant
to the needs of our time,"
Zelinsky concludes softly,
meditatively. Head ever
so slightly
tilted to one shoulder, he is all
heartfelt tenderness, forever
warm, sweet, and compliant.
We talk a little more, drink tea
with sugar, with small bagels.
And we sit there for a while,
eyes sliding over the bindings
of the books in the rich,
well-cared-for library
that resembles its owner.
Platonov gets to his feet.
I do the same.
We run—fly—hurtle
down the stairs
and wander for a long time
about Moscow.
There are a lot of cars.
Which are Black Marias,
we don't know. We don't
discuss this, but we know
we both think about it
and think about
how we both know this.
"And you? Can you
make out
what's relevant
to the needs of our time
and what isn't?"

Platonov asks, boldly,
on Bolshaya Ordynka.
I'm twenty years old. Wet
behind the ears. "No,"
I reply. I feel ashamed
of my answer, but it's the truth.
"Precisely!" A pause. A look.
A pause. "Stay like that.
Don't change." Platonov falls
silent, withdraws into himself,
then says, "In fifty years' time,
who knows, it may perhaps
become clear
what era you and I live in
and what name
should be given it. But,
more likely, it will
be given many different names—
some very strange—
chosen by the grandchildren
of those in power at this hour—
the grandchildren, I should say,
of everyone living today."

He was walking fast,
not looking from side
to side, holding his head
up high,
with its high cheekbones
and flinty chin.

*Translated by Robert Chandler*

# Reviews

## Eric

**Richard J. Evans, *Eric Hobsbawm: A Life in History*, Little, Brown, 2019, 798 pages, hardback ISBN9781408707418, £35**

Hobsbawm always insisted on 'Eric', so Eric he will be here. This is something of a departure for Evans, best known for his many books on Germany and Nazism, also for lethal testimony in the David Irving-Deborah Lipstadt trial. My uncorrected proof copy lacks both illustrations and bibliography. The latter can be excavated from the 81 pages of endnotes, meticulously source-documented plus extra information supplementary to the main narrative. The excellent 36-page Index (eight devoted to Eric) comports a list of his books.

Long life (95 years), so long book. Much value accrues from use of Eric's unpublished Diaries (mainly in German) and his multi-generic fugitive pieces. Complementary is Eric's memoir, *Interesting Times,* dubbed (page ix) by Stefan Collini as 'that interesting hybrid, an impersonal autobiography'.

This doorstopper is friendly (the two were well acquainted) but not a hagiography; Eric gets his fair share of flak, personal and political. Book-ended by provocative Preface and Conclusion, the ten, chronologically-arranged chapters come with nifty titles that shape a mini-biography: The English Boy; Ugly as Sin, but a Mind; A Freshman Who Knows About Everything; A Left-wing Intellectual in the English Army; Outsider in the Movement; A Dangerous Character; Paperback Writer (shared with the Beatles – Eric, though, detested all pop music); Intellectual Guru; Jeremiah; National Treasure.

Eric had a knack for chronological coincidences. Born 1917 (in Alexandria), he arrived in Berlin in 1931, saw the red light (had a brush with Stormtroopers), and made for England in 1933. Complex Jewish family (Evans disentangles well), complex schoolings in Vienna (already toxic with anti-Semitism), England ('dull'), and Berlin (his favourite: stimulating, classically-inclined and well-informed-in-Marxism teachers).

His ugliness evokes Sartre's (whom he knew and liked), made him diffident with women, to whom he came late. Evans even suggests Marxism was his sex substitute (page 75). His first marriage was a disaster, his second a triumph (wife Marlene a powerhouse in her own right), with Eric, the perfect husband and father, henceforth living in marital bliss.

Hard to believe (same with Marx) he ever took the *Manifesto's* proposed abolition of family seriously. Between the two, Eric had a surprising liaison with a drug-addicted young prostitute. Prime attraction, erotic services apart, was her love of jazz, Eric's other passion.

Tartly remarking he knew more about it than *Observer* guru Kingsley Amis (not applicable to fellow aficionado Philip Larkin), Eric became the *New Statesman's* jazz critic, the columns eventually published in book form under the name of Francis Newton, a communist drummer who had played on Billy Holiday's haunting *Strange Fruit* (about a lynching), whom Eric worshipped, writing a beautiful tribute after her death and hanging a photograph as sole mural decoration in his study.

Jazz was a maverick communist enthusiasm. In the Soviet Union (dutifully followed by the Communist Party of Great Britain), this music was routinely denounced as 'degenerate' and 'epileptic'; cf. Frederick Starr's *Jazz in the Soviet Union* (1983; rev. 2004). Eric explained his musical love affair in the *London Review of Books* (27 May 2010).

At Cambridge, start of a lifelong connection, he was a brilliant undergraduate (talent-spotted for different reasons by Noel Annan and James Klugmann), researcher (his work initially disliked by Postan and Tawney – there'd be eventual reconciliations), and lecturer. Election to The Apostles brought contact with Burgess and Blunt – both doubtless enjoyed Annan's paper on buggery more than Eric, but no evidence of complicity in their espionage. British (later also American) Intelligence was constantly sniffing around him, but they had nothing to fear. Eric was the classic academic armchair revolutionary. In the War, spent on educational work around England, he saw no action and was one of few not to volunteer for a dangerous Norwegian mission. Apart from some anti-Vietnam War demonstrating, he was no street fighter, nor did he do any of the routine CPGB chores (eg selling the *Daily Worker*). Typically, Intelligence missed the big fish ('Cambridge Five'), whilst Eric was farcically listed as a 'Dutch Jew' (page 702 note 187).

Post-war, Eric's academic star blazed ever brighter. He alternated between Cambridge and Birkbeck College, with a stream of lecture tours and visiting appointments in America and around the world, showing special affection for India and, naturally, Cuba. Hailed everywhere as a spellbinding lecturer and affable guest, his many books won plaudits even from anti-Marxists. Multifarious in interests and writing, Eric called himself primarily an economic historian. He singled out *Primitive Rebels* as his personal favourite – see my ' Ancient Socialism' (*Spokesman* 112, 2010) for his highlighting of revolutionary cobblers, whose modern loss of zeal he comically lamented. Unlike Evans, I greatly like his final work, *How to Change the World: Tales of Marx and Marxism* (2011) – see my lengthy review article on the ReadySteadyBook website (UK).

One criticism from all sides was Eric's neglect of nationalism. He eventually broke down and published *Nations and Nationalism*, deprecating all such parochial ideologies.

Another topic he studiously avoided was the Holocaust – 'not interested in the Shoah,' a Jewish relative disclosed. Eric's view seems to have been that it was one of many interconnected tragedies, not to be segregated for particular treatment.

Of course, *the* question always aimed at Eric was why stay in the CPGB after the 1956 Khrushchev denunciation of Stalin? When faced with this by Sue Lawley on *Desert Island Discs*, he feebly replied, 'we didn't know'. He'd only needed to ask Malcolm Muggeridge. Davenport-Hines quotes Eric's telling late-in-life admission that 'in early youth' he had developed 'a facility for deleting unpleasant or unacceptable data'.

In the 1930s, Eric had defended the show-trials, employing the standard 'Trotskyite wrecker' slur. He similarly sought to excuse the 1956/68 invasions of Hungary and Czechoslovakia. On the other hand, he dismissed Stalin's writings as 'dull', preferring the 'cheeriness' inspired in him by Lenin (surely a unique reaction), and had increasingly set himself at odds with such CPGB luminaries as John Gollan and George Matthews.

Why did the CPGB not expel Eric? He did no Party chores, and was routinely disparaged as a mere 'intellectual'. But the Party brass wanted to capitalize on his British and international fame (and fortune), so essentially put him in the Brecht/Yevtushenko category of 'licensed dissident'.

Eric's answer was obvious. Better to stay and work for changes within than rail uselessly from outside. One recalls US President Johnson's 'tent-pissing' explanation for re-appointing J. Edgar Hoover. *En passant*, one matter seemingly passed over by Evans is Eric's reaction to the Party's controversial 1951 manifesto *The British Way to Socialism,* discarding revolution for the ballot box. Edward Upward left in disgust (cf. my remarks in *Spokesman* 127, 2015.)

Eric had always denigrated Trotsky and followers, once branding them ' nightmarish'. Yet, had he resigned, might he have been seduced by Gerry Healey into the Trotskyite wasteland? If so, what? Think of Peter Fryer …

Of special interest to *Spokesman* readers is Eric's relationship to Ken Coates. In the *New Statesman* (November 1973) he praised Ken as 'the most under-rated political analyst among British Marxists today'. A decade later (*New Left Review*, January-February 1982), in his 'The Choices

Before Labour', Ken combined similar eulogies of Eric with sharp criticism of his views on Trade Unions. In a Diary entry for 7 November 1982, Tony Benn recorded Ken's reaction to Eric at a conference in Yugoslavia as becoming a centrist, flirting with the Social Democrat likes of Sue Slipman and company.

I could have filled this entire *Spokesman* issue with discussion of the myriad minutiae provided by Evans – by the end, I had amassed 50 pages of notes. Not many books can be described as, or remain, definitive. But, it is hard to imagine anyone improving on this one.

CODA. Several websites give lists of Eric's aphorisms. Apart from his characterization of Blair as ' Thatcher in trousers', here's my favourite:

> 'As the global expansion of Indian and Chinese restaurants suggests, xenophobia is directed against foreign people, not foreign cultural imports.'

Looking around Britain today, who could disagree?

*Barry Baldwin*

## Highlighting the weaknesses

**Lev Ozerov, *Portraits Without Frames*, Editors Robert Chandler and Boris Dralyuk, Granta 2019, 256 pages, ISBN 9781783784714, £14.99**

The Master of Revels in Pushkin's 'little tragedy' *A Feast in Time of Plague* (1830) undergoes, in the space of a few pages, and with a speed and deftness rivalling anything in Ozerov's *Portraits*, a complex transformation: from indomitable celebrant of the human capacity to defy crushing circumstance – the death carts pass by even as he rhapsodises the eternalising power of suffering – to one who, capsized by grief at the loss of his loved ones, 'remains, lost in thought'. His thought, our thought – Pushkin refuses to clarify or simplify the impact experience, impulse and emotion have had. But the Master's earlier Hymn ['Within each breath of death / lives joy, lives secret joy / for mortal hearts, a pledge / perhaps, of immortality, / and blessed is he who, storm-tossed, / can see and seize this joy'] has acquired in the light of that final image an almost fatuous edge, just as, a century later and in the icy grip of the Stalinist winter, the hollowness of the partygoers' hurrahs becomes in Akhmatova's *Voronezh* 'the poplars / rattle, like glasses ringing in a toast' while 'in the exiled poet's hideaway / the muse and terror fight their endless fight / throughout the night. / So dark a night will never see the day'. To pass from the Shakespearean pathos with which Akhmatova evokes the casual extermination of Osip Mandelstam (and simultaneously, the ongoing, decades-long assault on generations of the Soviet cultural elite), to the fifty vignettes that make up Ozerov's reconstruction in the 1990s of all that had been lost and needed, in his view, to be redeemed, is to be aware of a savage irony attending the collection's innocuous-sounding title: what other gallery of portraits in the history of literature or its sister arts could be more 'framed' by the cyclone of social and ideological convulsion?

Ozerov neither avoids nor dwells upon the horror. His focus, rather, like Pushkin's treatment of the Master, and as he avows in the portrait of Leyb Kvitko, one of thirteen members of the Jewish Anti-Fascist Committee who perished during the 'Night of the Murdered Poets', August 12 1952, is on selfhood, on what happens when each of his subjects is drawn forward into the spotlight, however fleetingly, *in propria persona*: 'a human being is an inexhaustible subject, / especially if his life / has been cut short'. The tributes to Kvitko and two further victims, Dovid Hofshteyn and Peretz Markish, carry one may argue – and might anticipate, from a fellow Jewish-Ukrainian — an additional weight of identification, affection, visceral outrage, Hofshteyn "the mildest man I ever knew", the "wild scream … In a voice not her own" of Esther Markish when the KGB offer to repay her for her dead husband's gold crowns. But one must look elsewhere for evidence of Ozerov's readiness to engage directly and unflinchingly with historical atrocity, to the topographical precision, eyewitness veracity and emotional power of his *Babi Yar* [1944-5], 'the longest Russian-language Shoah poem written and published in Stalin's time' [Maxim D. Shrayer]. 'Pleading, here at this place I stand. / If my mind can endure the violence, / I will hear what you have to say, land – / Break your silence.'

Joseph Brodsky characterises the Soviet interregnum as a dream of the rule of facelessness – 'bland, grey, undistinguished faces: they look like everyone else, which gives them an almost underground air; they are similar as blades of grass' – over ever-expanding numbers of the faceless – 'the depersonalisation and bureaucratization of everybody alive' [*On Tyranny*, 1980]. Instead, one by one, the stars of Ozerov's literary and artistic pantheon are glimpsed or remembered in scenes of trenchant self-revelation, furtive disclosure, or more rarely, like novelist Konstantin Paustovsky confronting Khrushchev's acolytes in the Writers' Union, vehement repudiation of the 'Dense-packed rows / of clean shaven faces

… he just pushed a boulder from his soul / and rolled it away'. There are instances where fascination with the aura of creative or intellectual pre-eminence, so beloved of the younger Ozerov – 'I listened to their [the architect Burov and formalist critic Shklovsky's] conversations / like a pre-schooler… spool after spool of unforgettable talk. / I'd won a lottery' – and never quite relinquished by his older self, manage to momentarily obliterate any more measured account of an individual's essential, perhaps contradictory humanity, but they are few and far between. The portrait of Burov is unremittingly glamorous ['He did nothing small / or petty, his whole life a grand / expenditure of time and energy. / Work, cognac, wives' …], and unremittingly satirical, but the explosive, visionary energy ['his boldness, his inborn joy / and desire for perfection'] and an instance of personal courage silence all criticism. Emil Gilels' tight-lipped acquiescence in his own exploitation, on the other hand, epitomised by a demeaning personal endorsement from Stalin, robs the sonic power of his pianism – 'an unbridled force of nature' – of some of its grandeur. But it's the all-but-invisible, all-but-indefinable inner torment of Gilels, caught listening to unprogrammable Bach in a secluded corner of Riga Cathedral, not Burov's epic self-sufficiency, that elicits Ozerov's compassion and lends itself more naturally to the pattern and method of these poems – self-effacement, ingratiation even, their author's extraordinary ubiquity, empathy or comradeship, and permanently raised antennae, sensitive to every chance encounter, gesture or utterance that might illuminate a given individual. How *did* he, one wonders, gain access to so many perilous confidences, in a society where, as Figes' *The Whisperers* has shown, trust had all but evaporated? Why is it to Ozerov the historian Irakly Andronikov chooses to unburden himself of the knowledge, on 5 March 1953, that not only Stalin but also Prokofiev has died? – 'I told you, / but, please, don't / tell anyone else'… Gilels stealing out from under the organ loft recalls the temporarily exiled Pasternak outside Svetitskhoveli Cathedral in Georgia, after a moment of private communion with the eleventh century, but whereas Pasternak recoils like a startled deer caught in someone's headlights when recognised by passers-by and bolts for cover, writes Ozerov, 'like Pushkin's Eugene / from the Bronze Horseman', Gilels 'looked around carefully, / saw me, and came up to me'.

The volume as edited closes with a rare exception to the round of celebrities: Ozerov's father. His gentle reproof 'when eyes like yours / gaze at this world's iron contours, / those contours blur and soften / into boughs of lilacs' suggests perhaps part of the reason Ozerov was able to provide such a goldmine of minute observation, here lovingly transcribed by the co-translators in an effort, not unlike Ozerov's own, to rescue the brilliant multi-facetedness of Soviet culture from the neglect and, frequently, opprobrium it has faced not just in its own land but also in the English-speaking world. The images solicit our attention tenderly and, except in extreme cases, non-judgementally, in a range of tones that run from unabashed candour [Akhmatova: 'A loose-fitting robe, or a housecoat / or, rather, a coverall / disguises her corpulence – / a gift of the prison queues'] to wild hilarity [Khachaturian returning humiliated from an abortive photo shoot with Salvador Dali: 'It is said that this episode / cooled the composer's ardour: / he went less often on tour / to dodgy venues']. In the final analysis, however, the murderous scythe still hangs in the air, whatever ingenuities a person adopts to evade it: one thinks of the early death of Mikhail Zoshchenko, alluded to by Ozerov, despite all the ironic games or narrative subterfuges that enabled his satires to reach their targets; or the decades-long, fulminating despair as Ozerov characterises it of Yuri Olesha, "unwanted writer", for refusing to disown the anarchic subversion of his early novella *Envy*. There are countless examples here. The wielders of the scythe are less often glimpsed, or pursued into their state-sanctioned lairs: Zelinsky, Kovpak, Zhdanov, Fadeyev. The latter's suicide during the Khrushchev thaw as a Stalin henchman and proponent of *Zhdanovschina* is the occasion for one of the most cautiously ambivalent portraits in the whole collection: 'Poor Sasha! … It's hard to write about Fadeyev'. One only has to compare this to Korney Chukovsky's 'Conscientious, talented, and sensitive as he was, he was floundering in oozy, putrid mud and drowning his conscience in wine' to sense the complexity of Ozerov's entirely characteristic restraint. Interestingly, Fadeyev is the one writer from *Portraits* whose name also appears on the list drawn up by the Russian Ministry of Education in response to Vladimir Putin's initiative, during the 2012 election campaign, calling for

'a canon of 100 Russian books that every school leaver will be required to read at home … State policy with regard to culture must provide appropriate guidelines … The government should also support literature because it always makes the most accurate diagnosis of society's condition and highlights its weaknesses.'

*Stephen Winfield*

## Academe politics

**Richard Clogg, *Greek To Me: A Memoir of Academic Life*, I.B.Tauris, 2018, 368 pages, hardback ISBN 9781784539887, £55.00**

Along with C. M. Woodhouse (deceased), Richard Clogg is the pre-eminent British historian of modern Greek history, attested by his many books and countless articles (eg 'Greek-Bashing,' *London Review of Books,* 18 August 1994), written during an often fraught academic career at Edinburgh, King's College London, and St. Antony's College Oxford.

Seven lengthy chapters, book-ended by Introduction and Epilogue, with 25 black and white illustrations, a mere two pages of end-notes, no bibliography, serviceable index, composed in Clogg's lucid prose, un-clogged by jargon for which he shows a healthy contempt extending to 'Political Correctness', richly laced with acerbic humour encompassing a multiplicity of targets personal and institutional.

As with all such memoirs, *Greek To Me* is inevitably self-serving apropos of Clogg's deep and passionate involvement in academic and political controversies, with much concomitant paying-off of old scores. This evokes the much quoted 'academic politics are so vicious because the stakes are so low,' usually attributed to Henry Kissinger, though Clogg (p. 4) credits Californian politico Jesse Unruh.

It is also one of the most conceited (with a degree of concomitant persecution-mania) books I've read, Clogg never missing a chance to quote favourable remarks and reviews at considerable length. Some may object to his disobliging remarks on female appearances, for instance (p. 51) that of Byzantinist Joan Hussey as 'frumpish and portly'.

Choice comic moments alleviate. Examples: Byzantinist R. M. Dawkins cackling from treetop; Birmingham classical professor failing to recognize a departmental colleague; American Judith Hallett who reported two rivals to the FBI as possible ' Unabomber' suspects — Clogg drily remarks, 'see how these classicists love one another' (Ahem!); Romanians relishing the chance to greet Michael Foot with ' Foot-Ceausescu' shouts, playing on their word 'Fut" (= 'Fuck'); Ceausescu's labrador (a gift from Liberal David Steel) with its military rank (Colonel), private food-taster, and monthly cash allowances. Other light moments include Arthur Scargill in Bulgaria complaining of poor restaurant service, 'if this is communism you can stuff it'; and the CIA's proposal to use killer mosquitoes in

Afghanistan — how did they distinguish friend from foe?

Greece is not Clogg's unique focus. There is a good deal on Romania, jubilantly hailing the Ceausescus' fall (their summary execution was broadcast on television on Christmas Day 1989), rightly excoriating British cuddling up to them, especially fierce on blithe acceptance of Elena the pseudo-scientist, her 'thesis' published by (Clogg's words) that other con artist, pseudo-Labour Robert Maxwell. Clogg also recounts a stint on building one of Enver Hoxha's new railways in Albania with student 'volunteers'.

For present purposes, chapters 2 and 3 are the most pertinent, respectively dealing with the 'Ruritanian' Greek Colonels' 1967-74 darkly-farcical regime and the troubles (largely manufactured by other personal and political vested interests, both British and Greek) Clogg encountered (and overcame) in his efforts to write a disinterested history of the *SOE* (Special Operations Executive — Clogg rightly laughing at this pompous title).

Clogg worked tirelessly to expose and undermine the junta, both organizationally and through multitudinous articles and speeches, working with many British and Greek fellow-opponents, ranging from Eleni Vlachou, editor of Greece's best newspaper *Kathimerini,* to *Private Eye*'s Paul Foot.

There was also a Swiftian battle of the books, with Clogg fiercely reviewing such pro-Colonels apologias as David Holden's (unindexed) *Greece Without Columns* and Kenneth Young's *The Greek Passion.* He does admit, though, that Classicist-reviewer Peter Green had a point in complaining about unique worldwide condemnation of the junta. People do have selective consciences. I think of the many present evils which elicit no street demonstrations.

The Labour Party does not come out of this well. MP Francis Noel-Baker cuddled up to the junta to protect his Greek properties. Another, Gordon Bagier, took cash retainers to provide favourable public relations. There's documentary evidence of the Government's friendly overtures to the military regime, plus Harold Wilson's cognate breezy dismissal of the Soviet invasion of Czechoslovakia as ' something to forgive and forget'.

I regret that leading archaeologist Spyridon Marinatos eagerly embraced the Colonels. Nemesis was quick — he was crushed to death during excavations by a collapsing wall.

Clogg (pages 91-94) could/should have said more about the murder of journalist Ann Chapman. The British Government refused to investigate. Turkish Intelligence (1978) maintained she was killed by the Greek Secret

Service at the CIA's behest. In the same year, Soviet defector Arkady Shevchenko described her death as 'sinister'. The man convicted of her rape and murder was released in 1983, declared innocent. For detailed investigation, see David Cade's *Athens — the Truth: Searching for Manos, Just Before the Bubble Burst* (2013, especially pages 154-55).

Ironic note: the Colonels subverted democracy. Their ancient Athenian equivalents twice rescued it from repressive oligarchies.

After a rehearsal of the obstacles placed in the way of his *SOE* history, Clogg continues with an updated re-run of his controversial *Politics and the Academy: Arnold Toynbee and the Koraes Chair*, a grisly account of Toynbee's unseating and consequent 'unperson' relegation in official King's College histories. This chair  was founded by a man who said reading Byzantine literature gave him gout. Toynbee owed his elevation to logrolling by Regius Professor of Greek, Gilbert Murray, his teacher and father-in-law. But he made the fatal mistake in Hellenic eyes by saying the Greeks were no better than the Turks in 1922 wartime atrocities. The consequent Greek vendetta against him was abetted by T. S. Eliot who dubbed Toynbee 'a noxious humanitarian'.

After Toynbee's dethroning, a battle-royal broke out between Clogg and the top Byzantinists, both sides wanting the Chair to protect their academic fiefdoms. Clogg, writing as the loser, discharges both barrels at rival luminaries. I know/knew all these personally, whereas I've never met Clogg.

After remarking that John le Carré alluded to St. Antony's as a training ground for spies, Clogg's *envoi* consists of printing his valedictory speech (its praise of *Lucky Jim* is a clear message) and laments over how cash-strapped universities increasingly truckle to cash blandishments from business, industry, and politicians, instancing Cambridge's Margaret Thatcher Professorship of Enterprise Studies — obviously wouldn't be Oxford. He perhaps overstates his case, but there is a case to be overstated – Clogg's quotation (page 272) of an unnamed American academic: 'only trouble with tainted money is that there t'aint enough of it'.

This *Memoir* is a thumping good read. According to personal prejudice and taste, it will elicit contrary views of Clogg. On the one hand, his anti-Colonels crusade was admirable, whilst in modern Greek history he is an unquestionable superstar. On the other, his tone is often that of a rancid, grudge-holding loser of sectarian battles. His own words, ' a dispiriting tale of academic intrigue', may say it all. I have never moved in high business or political circles, but after 50-some years graft in universities, I can vouchsafe the truth of the academic trenches. The stakes were not always trivial but, overall, Kissinger/Unruh was right.

*Barry Baldwin*

## Libya

**Rob Weighill and Florence Gaub,** *The Cauldron – NATO's Campaign in Libya*, **Hurst and Company, 2018, 388 pages, hardback ISBN 9781849048828, £40**

To read and understand how these multi-national projects and operations work, especially on the scale of mega-organizations like NATO and the UN, is fascinating and disturbing at the same time. I confess the military-security background of the authors and the recommendation by Peter Hain put me on the alert. And I was right to be wary – with some reservations because this is really a specialist read, or works if it is taken as such.

'Chaos' rather than 'Cauldron' would have perhaps been a better title because you get little idea of the violence on the ground – it is a little like watching all those Wrens pushing counters on a large table in front of serious men in blue to describe the blood, fear and fury of a battle in the air as so often seen in World War Two movies. Yet, the sense of chaos is palpable in the corridors of power, trying to coordinate not only NATO and the UN but also The League of Arab States, the Organization of the Islamic Conference and The African Union, along with contending political agendas, not to speak of politicians' egos. For a start, there was basic ignorance about Libya and confusion about Gaddafi himself. First, he had been the bad guy, the backer of terrorism (responsible for the Lockerbie plane bombing, though surely there are still unanswered questions about that) and then he was a good guy entertaining the likes of Sarkozy and Blair and giving up his weapons of mass destruction – a lesson surely not lost on Rocket Man. But when the Arab Spring back-footed Gaddafi, NATO was equally unprepared, with staff shortages and vital officers on leave or on training exercises. NATO was under American command but the commander was busy with American forces, so it fell to a Canadian, Charles Bouchard, who is one of the few to come out of this sorry business with any credit, sticking to the remit of UN resolutions and resisting as far as possible the pressures of politicians to get tougher and rougher. That happened anyway – it was all supposed to start nice and gentle, to prevent a Rwanda-type slaughter, though there is little evidence that there was any such danger. However, it was claimed, the motive was 'humanitarian', to protect civilians. Who these civilians were is somewhat vague because where did the opposition come from if not from 'ordinary people'? There were plenty of them, right enough, but Al-Qaeda/ Nusra inspired groups, seeing a golden opportunity, quickly moved in. And surely Iraq should have made the powers-that-be wary of oppositions in exile, not necessarily brave fighters for their country's freedom, but then, of course, the powers-that-be probably knew exactly what they were doing; plenty of experience, after all.

So a free-fly zone and an arms embargo were initiated. How this was interpreted varied from so much 'humanitarianism' that it was like trying to fight a war without anyone getting hurt to heavy violence. What if you kill civilians you are supposed to be protecting if it will later prevent the greater loss of civilian lives? Do you only bomb armaments factories or bomb the hell out of everything – infrastructure and transport and everything that might facilitate their movement and the arming of the enemy? And there you have it, like it or not, things escalate and get out of hand and, for all the stated good intentions of not taking sides, NATO ends up backing one side. And 'Regime Change', which is supposed to be off the menu, is suddenly back on it. The rebels were in control of the air and, against all the stated rules, arms were run to them; furthermore, there were 'boots on the ground' – page 207 refers to 'the continued presence of advisers on the ground'. We have all heard that one before; the question is how many advisers do you have to have before you start calling them 'troops' or 'soldiers'.

The aftermath of Gaddafi's downfall is well known from his obscene death and gloating laughter of Hillary Clinton, to the splits which quickly appeared between members of the National Transitional Council and the countries which had originally supported and/or recognized it, not to mention the appalling levels of violence ever since. *The Cauldron*, in its conclusion, touches on all this and does not deny NATO's mistakes and faults, but its authors essentially support and believe in the operation. For all the research (and of its 388 pages, 131 are Notes, Bibliography and Index) the pro-Western tone is unmistakable: Lavrov, Russia's foreign minister, 'fumes' and Saif al-Islam, one of Gaddafi's sons, calls the International Criminal Court a 'Mickey Mouse court'. The ICC's prosecutor said he had 'direct evidence' that he, his father and brother-in-law had 'formed an inner circle that crushed peaceful demonstrations and ordered the use of live ammunition and heavy weapons against protesters'. They may or may not have done so, but Israel anyone? One can never escape the feeling that double standards are applied along with a good dose of hypocrisy: one rule for them, another for us; we always behave honourably, 'they' always behave badly – except they don't always. Early on, the authors write,

'The [Libyan] state invested heavily in infrastructure and welfare; literacy rates rose up to 90% ... health care was free and housing was heavily subsidised. Libya improved on most good governance criteria – such as the rule of law, regulatory quality, corruption control ...'

Quite an achievement by any standard but probably not 'in our interests' and, indeed, Professor Horace Campbell of Syracuse University says the real motive was to cause instability in the region rather than prevent it. This may be difficult for the average consumer of British and American popular media to accept or understand.

I watched the whole business unfold on Hugo Chavez's Telesur, always quickly dismissed as propaganda, which it is, but no more so and probably less when it comes to reporting on international affairs than the BBC or CNN. (Tariq Ali had his own excellent weekly programme, too.) Hugo Chavez hated the Americans and with good reason (they tried to regime-change him) and offered Gaddafi refuge in Venezuela. Chavez was then participating in a kind of Latin American 'Arab Spring', with Rafael Corea of Ecuador, Evo Morales of Bolivia, Lula and Dilma of Brazil, the Castros in Cuba, the Sandinistas in Nicaragua, the Kirchners in Argentina, even Juan Manuel Santos of Colombia,  the once hard-line minister of war under the corrupt and murderous Uribe, who was negotiating with the FARC. Every single Latin American country and many other countries on other continents well know that the Americans (and the French and the British) have *never* acted on a political level out of 'humanitarian' motives, rather they have supported and bought to power dictators far worse than Gaddafi whose human rights records were/are far worse than his.

One final word on this interesting but very flawed book: there are a number of misprints that need to be corrected for future editions; a few more detailed  maps would have been useful; and the editors need to get their *Thesaurus* out – I lost count of the times the phrase 'pushed back' was used in the sense of 'disagreed' rather than military resistance.

*Nigel Potter*

## Hugo Blanco

Hugo Blanco, *We the Indians – The Indigenous peoples of Peru and the struggle for land*, with a foreword by Eduardo Galeano, Merlin Press, 2018, 198 pages, paperback ISBN 978850367386 £15.99

Derek Wall, *Hugo Blanco A revolutionary for life*, Merlin Press, 2018, 144 pages, paperback ISBN 9780850367485, £14.99

*We the Indians* improves as it goes along. Hugo Blanco's own political vision develops and he becomes more 'Indian', his early Trotskyism broadens into eco-revolution, and the peasant and countryside are as important as the urban, industrialised working class. This is a big shift. If it is right and proper to demand that workers in sweatshops be allowed the right to unionise, or to mourn the loss of community when a coalmine or steelworks closes down, it is surely necessary to understand that working in a sweatshop or down a mine or in a steelworks in no way represents 'the good life'. The right to work is all very well but what kind of work are we talking about? Is it dangerous and dirty? Is it really necessary (something that satisfies basic human needs?) or does it destroy the human spirit? The 'lazy' life of the 'primitive' is to the unprejudiced eye often much more civilised and enjoyable than the lives of what Thoreau called 'lives of quiet desperation'. Our own consumer societies are not happy ones.

Much of this is described in Derek Wall's biography of Blanco, which is by far the better read. It is something of a hagiography, the great revolutionary who can do no wrong in his ceaseless search for social justice, but it gives a much better idea of the man's dedicated and often dangerous struggle. Hugo Blanco has many more than the cat's proverbial nine lives and his survival does seem extraordinary. After all, it is not difficult to kill an activist: ride up on a motorbike, pillion passenger with gun ready, bang-bang you're dead, and roar away. The thing is the Peruvian regimes were, for all their atrocities, never 100% evil. There were a few honest judges and even police chiefs sympathetic to the aims of the revolutionaries, and it's made very clear that national and international solidarity did and does or can make a huge difference. Some regimes even had left leanings (Juan Velasco's) but Hugo Blanco opposed them as well and, in Velasco's case, lost the support even of the Cubans who supported Velasco.

Hugo Blanco did become a more conventional politician for short periods, when he admits to strategic and tactical errors, but he was never comfortable in such roles. He is a born oppositionist, and one wonders whether he could ever handle the responsibilities of power. Deals and compromises have to be made, and it can be difficult to find the balance between doing that and selling out revolutionary principles. Perhaps people like Blanco in permanent opposition are necessary as watchdogs. He was on the death lists of Fujimori's dictatorship and the Shining Path revolutionaries, whom Blanco likened to Pol Pot's Khmer Rouge.

With his growing admiration and respect for the 'Indian Way of Life', Blanco would likely argue that power politics as we know them are unnecessary. He rejects what we call 'democracies' as being nothing of the kind, but a different version of the old game of elites bossing the plebs about. They have all the power and it takes a hell of an effort to break it. Perhaps it is only to be expected that, having devoted his whole life to revolutionary change, Blanco sees some improvement and progress, but I think he is overly optimistic here. The plight of the Indians everywhere throughout the American continent remains dire. Even sincere and honest indigenous leaders such as Evo Morales of Bolivia are forced to continue with the rape of Mother Earth in the teeth of indigenous opposition by encouraging and permitting mining interests to have their way for 'the sake of the economy'. It is true that the beginning of this century saw some real solidarity in Central and South America against the power of the world's biggest rogue state, the USA: the Kirchners in Argentina, Chavez in Venezuela, Correa in Ecuador, Lula and Dilma in Brazil, Morales in Bolivia, Mujica in Uruguay, the Sandinistas in Nicaragua, and the Castros in Cuba, but that movement is now in disarray.

The 'Indian Vision' described by both authors is perhaps the only real alternative we have. It's a pipe dream, one is accused of naivety even contemplating it, and it also has to be asked, 'what is the Indian Vison?' The Indians come in all shapes and sizes; some were as awful as any of their conquerors and oppressors. Even the authors admit that the Incas had their faults while denying they had an 'empire'. It is difficult to know what else to call the Inca 'empire', even if it was more benevolent than most. Indeed, much of the success of the *conquistadores* was due to the support they received from other tribes that hated the Aztecs so much. The Mayan 'civilisation' collapsed long before the arrival of the Spanish, probably because of environmental abuse and because 'the People' got so bloody tired of building all those pyramids for priests, princes and kings, not to mention their own internal wars.

That a non-Indian such as Hugo Blanco has listened to and acted on such a message is inspiring. I would like to have learned more about him though. There is a photo of him, age 80 years, with his six adult children, all smiling. What was the price they all paid for his activism, his long absences in exile and prison? What makes such a man tick? It's not just a gossipy interest because, in true Indian fashion, you cannot divorce the personal from the political.

*Nigel Potter*

*Nigel Potter was one of the founders of Proyecto Independiente de Salud Indigena Lenca (PISIL – Independent Lenca Indian Health Project) and worked for several years with the Central Nacional de los Trabajadores del Campo (CNTC – National Council for rural Workers), the largest campesino/peasant organization in Honduras.*

# Become a subscriber ...

# The Spokesman

Journal of the *Bertrand Russell Peace Foundation*

Subscription rates are (for three issues): Individual subscriptions: £20, Individual subscriptions - international: £25, Institutional subscriptions UK - £33 Europe - £38 RoW - £40.

Please send me one subscription, starting with Issue No. ............

I enclose payment of £ ............

Name...............................................................................................

Address

.........................................................................................................

.........................................................................................................

.........................................................................................................

.............................................................Postcode ......................

Email...............................................................................................

Please return this form with a cheque or money order made payable to 'Bertrand Russell House'. Send to The Spokesman, 5 Churchill Park, Nottingham, England, NG4 2HF.

Payments can be made online at the following websites:
**www.spokesmanbooks.com | www.spokesmanbookshop.com**